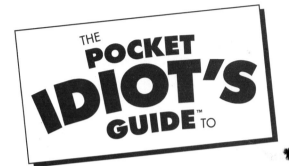

Health Savings Accounts

by Edie Milligan Driskill

D1570286

ALPHA

A member of Penguin Group (USA) Inc.

ALPHA BOOKS

Published by the Penguin Group

Penguin Group (USA) Inc., 375 Hudson Street, New York, New York 10014, U.S.A.

Penguin Group (Canada), 10 Alcorn Avenue, Toronto, Ontario, Canada M4V 3B2 (a division of Pearson Penguin Canada Inc.)

Penguin Books Ltd, 80 Strand, London WC2R 0RL, England

Penguin Ireland, 25 St Stephen's Green, Dublin 2, Ireland (a division of Penguin Books Ltd)

Penguin Group (Australia), 250 Camberwell Road, Camberwell, Victoria 3124, Australia (a division of Pearson Australia Group Pty Ltd)

Penguin Books India Pvt Ltd, 11 Community Centre, Panchsheel Park, New Delhi— 110 017, India

Penguin Group (NZ), cnr Airborne and Rosedale Roads, Albany, Auckland 1310, New Zealand (a division of Pearson New Zealand Ltd)

Penguin Books (South Africa) (Pty) Ltd, 24 Sturdee Avenue, Rosebank, Johannesburg 2196, South Africa

Penguin Books Ltd, Registered Offices: 80 Strand, London WC2R 0RL, England

To my children, Will and Lydia Milligan Delphia,
whose health and happiness are everything to me.

Contents

Introduction

My grandfather and his brother were the surgeons at the local hospital in Sidney, Ohio, in the 1950s. Sidney had about 15,000 people back then. If any one of them needed a surgery, they got it. If they didn't have the money, they paid for it later. Sometimes friends chipped in or my grandfather and great uncle did it for free. Even with their generosity, the brothers were still able to afford to live in the biggest houses on the highest hill in town.

The day my grandfather quit his practice was the day that his malpractice insurance premium went up to $1,000. He had never been sued. The people in Sidney depended upon him for their lives. The practice of medicine used to be a profession, but in my grandfather's and many others' eyes, it was quickly becoming a business run by lawyers and insurance companies. The hospital wouldn't let my grandfather perform surgery without the insurance. He was too old for such silliness, so he closed up shop.

Imagine his outrage if he were alive today. It seems like everyone is getting into the business of medicine: the businessmen, the politicians, the insurance companies, and now the bankers. Doctors are now forced to be businessmen selling a product, instead of professionals caring for the ill.

Health care has become one of the most debated topics in Washington and state capitals around the country. It seems that everyone has a problem with the current system. Most agree that it is broken, but few agree on what the solution should be. Private health insurance, one of the funding mechanisms for health care, has come under close scrutiny. Many believe that more people should be covered by an insurance contract, while others believe that the comprehensive coverage people have enjoyed has actually caused part of the problem of rising costs.

Small employers are caught right in the cross fire. Most working Americans receive their health insurance coverage through their (or their spouse's) employer. And most employees work for small companies. This leaves the small employer as the decision maker and on the front line of this battle.

Congress has been front and center in this debate. There isn't a member of Congress who hasn't listened to horror story after horror story from small employers fed up with the system. In the 2004 presidential campaign, President Bush and his opponents spoke of the health care crisis all along the campaign trail. At every opportunity, the president reminded voters of one of the key steps that Congress and he had already taken, creating Health Savings Accounts, or HSAs.

For most people listening to those speeches, the term HSA went in one ear and out the other. Insurance companies were just beginning to bring their high deductible plans to the market, and the banks were still plowing through the mounds of regulations from the Treasury Department, trying to decide whether it was worth it to offer HSAs at all.

A few years earlier, Congress had passed a law creating (Archer) Medical Savings Accounts. They were born out of an attempt to create something like the Health Savings Accounts we now have. But politics being what it is, the compromises and concessions watered them down to the point that (1) virtually no one qualified for them, and (2) virtually no bank wanted to offer them.

The backers of the concept waited a few years and watched the political tide. When they felt they could win some of the concessions back, they set out to fix Medical Savings Accounts. Again, politics being what it is, they felt they had a better chance starting fresh with a new name, so Health Savings Accounts were born. Like most second born, the rules are not as strict. Health Savings Accounts have many of the same features of Medical Savings Accounts, but without most of the problems.

It isn't important, at this point, to understand Medical Savings Accounts. If you had one, you were one of the chosen few, and your money can move to an HSA. If you didn't have one, you can now have an HSA, and this book will walk you through the steps of putting one into place.

If all politics is local, then all health care is personal. During my years as a financial counselor, I listened to countless individuals share their views on their personal health and how to fund their needs in that area. For some, it was their responsibility to take care of themselves by not smoking, eating right, and exercising. For others, they were only concerned with making sure their company had the perfect health insurance plan. And for many, it was clearly their doctor's responsibility to order the right test to make sure they didn't have a dread disease. These varying attitudes were revealed in how they managed their lifestyle choices, employee benefit options, and savings levels.

You probably know someone who has had a heart attack but who still smokes. You also probably know someone who runs 5 miles every day and has never touched cigarettes. Should they both pay the same premium for health insurance? Should they both have access to the same policies? Should an employer be allowed to fire the heart attack victim when he causes a 40 percent increase in the company's health insurance rates next year?

If you have answers to these questions, you are smarter than I am. In our hearts we always want people to have access to the health care they need. But when we consider our checkbooks, we want to pay what is fair for our own care, based on our own lifestyle. If I'm young and healthy, do I want my health-care dollars paying for care for older, more costly individuals? Probably not, if I can help it.

The question here is one of pooling, which is an insurance industry term that defines how we share the risk of potential expenses. Back in Sidney, my grandfather unofficially pooled the costs of everyone who needed surgery in town that year. Enough people paid him to cover his expenses and maintain his lifestyle that others could receive his services at reduced or no cost. He was willing to hold on to the risk of a malpractice lawsuit himself, but the hospital wanted him to pool his risk with other doctors by paying $1,000 into an insurance company, which would hold the money and return much more to him if he got sued.

Buying health insurance is pooling your money with others who have similar needs for health care. Paying into Medicare is pooling your money with every other working American to fund your future need for health care when you retire or should you ever become disabled. Paying income taxes is pooling your money to fund the health care of lower income individuals through Medicaid and other social welfare programs. Unlike all these other forms of insurance, when you fund a Health Savings Account, you are holding on to a portion of that risk yourself.

The lines have become blurred between insurance and social welfare programs. They are also fuzzy between public and private programs. While all these changes were happening, the medical services industry has been aggressively finding new ways to prevent, treat, and cure medical problems. We have more services to pick from than ever before—but we crave even more. We are spending a higher percentage of our collective income on medical services than ever before, and we are complaining loudly about it.

As you read this book, reflect on services that you and your loved ones have received in the last five years. Did your great-grandparents have MRIs?

Cholesterol medicine? New knees? We want access to these newly available tests and treatments. We want our insurance contracts to pay for them. But when we learn what they cost indirectly through our premiums and payroll taxes, we complain.

HSAs are one piece of a much larger puzzle that is beginning to bring this picture back into focus for us. Because they are rooted in sound economic theory, they have a hope of keeping costs down and helping us allocate our resources where we truly value them. They have the potential of sparking system-wide change because they begin where health care begins, with very personal decisions: What will my paycheck look like? How much will I save on taxes? What doctor can I go to? How much money can I save toward retirement goals? As you and your employees answer these questions, you will find out whether HSAs solve your personal health-care funding problems. And you will be participating in one of the most important national dialogues of the decade.

How to Use This Book

This book guides you through the process of understanding the concepts of High Deductible Health Plans and Health Savings Accounts. It gives you strategies beyond what a single insurance company will offer you, because it addresses the issues from your perspective as a small business owner.

You'll find a discussion of the philosophy behind the HSA concept in Chapter 1, followed by the nuts and bolts of the two contracts in Chapters 2 and 3. Chapter 4 unravels the new tax issues you will need to understand. Chapters 5 and 6 take you shopping for the contracts. Chapters 7 and 8 bring you back to what this means to you and your employees, as you design the optimal plan for your company. Chapter 9 recaps every step you will need to take in more detail. Chapter 10 applies the new approach to your and your employees' personal financial planning goals. We'll finish in Chapter 11 with a discussion of how Health Reimbursement Arrangements and Flexible Spending Accounts may offer you additional strategies.

The newness of Health Savings Accounts predicts their ongoing evolution and refinement. This book lays the groundwork for the concepts as they exist in mid-2005. I've given you resources throughout the appendices that can help you build on your basic knowledge and strategic understanding.

Extras

Throughout the book, I've included sidebars that provide definitions of health insurance terms, strategic tips, pitfalls to watch out for, and deeper insight into the concepts discussed.

Word Doctor _____

The insurance industry and Health Savings Accounts come with their own jargon. Here you'll find definitions for every new term you come across.

Premium Advice _____

Use these ideas to expand the value of these new products in your employee benefit or personal financial planning.

HSA Hazards _____

Beware of these concerns as you develop your own strategies.

Insurance Insights _____

Dig a little deeper into the concepts with these sidebars that help you understand the bigger picture.

Acknowledgments

I would like to thank my colleagues, Kevin Conrad of Rogers Benefits, Terry Smith of Avalon Benefits, and Scott Lewis of May Insurance, for their on-going support and encouragement of this book. Their insight as they read text, checked facts, and offered ideas was invaluable.

I owe much of my excitement about HSAs to my cousin, Bill Greenlee, owner of ROI Realty, who signed up for HSAs two weeks before his insurance company issued their first HDHP contract. He let me watch his thought process and learn from his employees what was needed to help them make the transition.

I want to acknowledge all the small business owners I have worked with over the past year, some of whom installed HDHPs and some of whom did not. From them, I learned when and how this new strategy would work. Specifically, Michael Silberstein deserves a mound of credit for introducing me to the most frustrated business owners in town.

A sincere thanks goes out to all the insurance company representatives who provided me data and insight as this book unfolded. Specifically helpful were Tom Richards from Cigna, Rob Guilbert from Assurant, Ellen Laden from Golden Rule, and Daryl Richard from UnitedHealthcare.

John Greene from the National Association of Health Underwriters filled me in on the political skinny and the possible future of HSAs.

Thanks go to Mike Sanders at Alpha Books and his wonderful team including Jan Lynn, Jennifer Moore, and Jeff Rose. This is our sixth book together. Mike continues to find new ways to make the process exciting and enjoyable.

Last, but never least, to my new husband, Allen Driskill, who has supported me throughout this new turn in my career. We got married somewhere between Chapters 3 and 4. I will always remember this book fondly.

Trademarks

Chapter 1

We're Consumers Again

In This Chapter

- What consumer-driven health care is all about
- An overview of High Deductible Health Plans
- An introduction to Health Savings Accounts

When you first heard the term *Health Savings Account*, what did you think? Another scheme by the insurance companies to complicate your life and make more money for themselves? A smoke screen from Congress to cover up the fact that they really have no idea how to fix our broken health-insurance industry? Or just another employee benefit strategy that leaves business owners out in the cold?

Your skepticism is truly justified. Insurance companies are for-profit corporations with unnecessarily complicated contracts. Congress is very confused and frustrated about how to contain spiraling health-insurance costs. And most employee benefit programs that provide tax relief to employees do not allow the owners to participate.

Not Your Father's Health Insurance

I can only imagine your shock as you learn that with High Deductible Health Plans, insurance companies actively encourage you to buy less insurance. And Congress gives you back both your income tax and Social Security/Medicare contributions (FICA) on HSA deposits to encourage you to open an HSA. And the biggest surprise: politicians are so eager to have companies make this change that they have included business owners in most of the tax savings.

When things don't add up, there is usually a catch. There is a big one with Health Savings Accounts: patients need to be consumers again. Many alert economists have noticed that the rising cost of health insurance has been driven by the rising cost of health care. They have concluded that health-care costs have risen due to an increasing demand for services from people who have no idea what these services really cost. In order to contain these costs, patients need to be well informed.

Learning what HDHPs and HSAs can do and how to choose the best strategy for yourself and your employees are the first steps to participating in the premium savings and tax benefits offered by these plans. Let's start with the basic strategy.

Insurance Insights

Finer restaurants used to have two menus: one with prices and one without. Men would see what their date's meal would cost but their date would not. The idea was that the women should order what they want, without any concern about the cost. Employers have been taking their employees to this restaurant for too long and are now horrified when the waiter brings the check.

Insurance Plus Savings

Back in the good ol' days, health insurance was sold as two separate contracts. The first, often known as Basic Health Insurance, covered doctor visits, lab tests, drugs, and other lower cost items. The other was known as Major Medical or Hospitalization. It covered the unforeseen big problems. A remnant of this system can be seen in the Medicare program, in which Part A is the Hospitalization and Part B is the Basic coverage.

During the 1970s, these two contracts began to be combined and sold as products cleverly called Basic plus Major Medical. The combined products that we have today, like HMOs (Health Maintenance Organizations) and PPOs (Preferred Provider Organizations), evolved out of this marriage.

We have lost touch with the notion that we are really funding two very different things when we buy health insurance: (1) predictable, ongoing, usually lower cost items and (2) unpredictable, major events costing thousands of dollars.

Let's take a peek at the car insurance industry for a clearer view of what has happened to health insurance. Consider why car-insurance companies don't pay for oil changes. Imagine having to send in proof that it really has been 3 months or 3,000 miles in order to get your claim paid. Then imagine having to prove that you used the right grade of oil suitable for your car and your climate? Your $29 oil change just went up to $45 to pay for all the time the claims adjuster spent to determine the appropriateness of paying your claim, the time the BestLube employee spent to fill out the paperwork to get reimbursed for their services, and time the actuaries spent to calculate the true probability that there will be three months happening in the next three months.

Isn't it easier to put $29 in your checking account and give them your debit card to pay for the oil change yourself? Some people actually spend $18 at BestAutoParts for the oil and filters and change the oil themselves. Would you get dirty to save $11? Maybe you would, but that's your choice. You are a consumer and you can make that decision rationally.

Car insurance companies are very good to have around when you wreck your car. Similarly, health-insurance companies are very good to have around when you wreck your body. But just as it would be highly inefficient to have your auto insurance pay for your oil changes, it's similarly inefficient to have your health-insurance company cover your regular checkups and other low-costs health-care expenses. We need another strategy for those ongoing, predictable, lower cost items. And now we have one … Health Savings Accounts. Bank accounts are much more efficient for the items we can predict and manage for ourselves. The insurance contracts are very efficient at pooling our risk of having something major happen that we can't afford to pay for with savings.

High Deductible Health Plans

Let's start with the notion that less insurance is better. Insurance companies have one key role in our economy and your lives. They pool risks. They take a bunch of people with the same potential risk for something and collect a portion of the potential loss from each person (the premium). When someone in the group experiences a loss, they distribute the money (the claim).

Word Doctor

Underwriting is the process of selecting people for the pool. If they select someone to be in the pool who has a higher risk for that loss, they will charge a higher premium.

If you are a male you have no risk of becoming pregnant. Agreed? Most of us understand that part of risk. The other end of the scale is more confusing. If you are a diabetic you have no risk of getting diabetes. When there is certainty at either end of the spectrum there is no risk.

Actuaries, the folks who spend their days calculating risks for insurance companies, can look at a large group of people and tell us the probability that one of them will become pregnant this year or that one of them will develop diabetes this year. With those probability factors and knowledge of what it costs to be pregnant or have diabetes, they can calculate a premium to charge everyone in that group.

Calculating the costs of certainties is a different exercise. If a group of males wanted insurance to pay for pregnancy the premium would be $0, because the risk is zero. If a group of diabetics wanted insurance to pay for their costs of managing that disease and its side effects, the premium would be the actual cost of services. In both of these cases, there is no reason to buy an insurance contract.

Insurance contracts work when there is risk. Think about car insurance. What if only car owners who already had damage to their cars bought insurance? The cost would be the cost of the repair. Car insurance works because we pay premiums before our teenager drives the car into the side of the garage.

This is where health insurance got complicated and expensive. It moved into the realm of paying for things that were already certainties. Regular checkups and preventive medications are routinely covered by insurance contracts now. As a financial vehicle, insurance doesn't work very well for those types of expenses. Savings works much better. So less insurance is better when it is combined with a savings plan to fund the predictable expenses.

The insurance contracts now being offered alongside Health Savings Accounts are called High Deductible Health Plans, or HDHPs for short. You can buy HDHPs from almost every health-insurance company in the country, and I'll help you evaluate your options in Chapter 5. If you have an HDHP in force, your employees qualify to open Health Savings Accounts (HSA), but there is no requirement that they do so. They could, if they wanted, fund these lower expenses through their weekly paycheck, a regular savings account, a credit card, or their parents (assuming they still love them).

Insurance Insights

Individuals do not need to be part of a group to purchase an HDHP or HSA. A list of insurance companies that sell individual policies is in Appendix C. Employers may only help pay for the premiums of group policies as a deductible employee benefit, however.

An HDHP is defined by the Internal Revenue Service (IRS) as a health-insurance plan with a minimum $1,050 deductible ($2,100 for a family). There can be no benefits paid before that $1,050 is met, with a couple of exceptions at this time. This means that a plan that has a co-payment of $20 for an office visit or a drug card that provides prescription benefits before the deductible is met would not qualify. Many insurance companies offer plans with high deductibles but still require co-payments for office visits and prescriptions. Technically, these are high deductible plans, but they do not meet the criteria to be considered an HDHP for the purpose of qualifying to open an HSA.

If you have an HMO or low deductible ($0–$500) PPO in place right now and you switch to an HDHP you will usually be buying less insurance. Therefore, your premium will usually go down. How far it drops depends on your current coverage amount and the make up of your employee group. In most of the situations you will save money on your insurance premium and on taxes. This is where you and your employees find the money to fund the savings accounts. Of course, you will need to decide who contributes to the accounts and how often. I'll walk you through these issues in Chapter 8.

Health Savings Accounts

Health Savings Accounts are not insurance contracts. They do not pool any risks. They accumulate money in the name of an individual for the purpose of paying for ongoing, smaller expenses related to health care. They are primarily offered by banks and investment companies. Some insurance companies also offer them, but usually through their subsidiaries or partners that are (guess what) banks or investment companies.

Insurance brokers all over the country are calling on their clients to offer them HSA options. What they are really offering are the HDHP options that allow employees to open HSAs. It's important to understand this distinction because more insurance companies are bundling the two contracts together in their marketing material. As you investigate these options remember that the employer purchases the HDHP and the employees own their own HSAs. You can recommend an HSA trustee to your employees and make it attractive by putting money in it for them, but ultimately the management of that account will be theirs and they can move it wherever they choose.

 HSA Hazards

Many financial services are now bundled—such as mortgages and mortgage insurance; car purchases and car financing; and life insurance and investments. Sometimes the fees for one are hidden inside the cost of the other. Make sure when you evaluate HDHPs and HSAs that you understand the cost of each.

The best way to think about an HSA is to start with what you know about Individual Retirement Accounts (IRAs). An IRA is in an individual's name and is held by a trustee. There is a yearly limit on contributions. Only certain people are allowed to have them. You have to pay taxes and penalties if you take the money out at the wrong time or for the wrong reason. You are limited as to what kind of investments you can choose for the funds. With this general context you can begin to apply the specific rules of HSAs.

To qualify to open an HSA, an individual must meet the following criteria:

- They must be covered by an HDHP (as defined by the IRS).
- They cannot be claimed as a dependent on someone else's tax return or be over 64 years old.
- They cannot be covered by Medicaid, Medicare, or another health plan that is not an HDHP.

So if you are under 65, claim yourself on your taxes, and are only covered by HDHPs, you're eligible. Unlike IRAs and 401(k)s, there are no income or ownership tests. You may make as much money as you like and own as much of the company as you do. As a highly paid owner or key employee, you also can open an HSA and deposit the maximum every year.

Premium Advice

Unlike the HSA side of this equation, there are no rules defining who can be covered by an HDHP. If you have employees over 65 or on Medicare, they can still have the insurance coverage. They just can't open the accompanying savings account.

HSAs share some of an IRA's tax treatment. The money you deposit is an above the line adjustment to your gross income. This means that it is subtracted from your total income before you calculate your itemized or standard deduction. The interest you earn will not be taxed. But unlike traditional IRAs, the money is not taxed when you withdraw it, as long as you spend it on qualifying medical expenses and certain insurance premiums. We'll go through the exact tax treatment of the deposits, the interest, and the withdrawals, as well as any forms you may need, in Chapter 4.

Insurance vs. Benefits

Your customers pay you. You pay your employees, your suppliers, and your overhead. The IRS asks you to pay tax on the difference. Seems simple enough, but then the world came up with complicated ways you can pay your employees. We've come a long way since workers lined up on Friday afternoon at the payroll office to get their week's wages in cold hard cash.

The Value of Benefits

What happened? Why did workers begin to request their income in a form other than cash on the spot? Even vacation pay baffles me. Why would a worker voluntarily ask to have a portion of their wages garnished this week so that they can ask for it back the week or two they get off work during the year? Do they really think they are "earning" that money while sunning on the beach?

Sometimes when a group of people joins together to buy something they qualify for discounts or achieve higher levels of efficiency, and this was the rational for the earliest group health-insurance products. Insurance companies could market more efficiently, spread around risk more effectively and therefore, offer a lower premium. Employers realized that health insurance was something that employees valued and, by offering it as a perk (remember that word?), they could attract a better workforce.

Group products also made it possible for employees who could not meet the underwriting qualifications for individual health-insurance contracts to get insurance by joining a group, where the requirements were lessened. This reality has caused an interesting reversal in the rating of individual products compared to group products. In many cases a healthy individual can pay less for an individual plan than it would cost to include them on a group plan. It is becoming more difficult for small employers to encourage young, healthy workers to join their groups. The new HDHP plans are a good strategy to keep costs down and participation up on small employer groups.

Whose Money Is It?

With all these issues at play, the term *benefit* becomes a little fuzzy. Is the benefit of employer-provided health insurance just the premium paid by the employer, in lieu of cash compensation? Or is it the access to an insurance plan that an employee could not purchase or qualify for on his or her own?

Insurance Insights

As an employer for 20 years, I interviewed a lot of potential employees. I was often asked, "Do you offer benefits?" " Sure!" I'd reply, "You get to wear jeans, work on a bus line, and eat lunch for free on Friday." The frowns on their faces told me they were really asking, "Do you have health insurance?"

This entire question is muddied by the notion that some of the premium is paid for by the employer and some by the employee at most companies. From the employer's perspective, it is all the employee's money. It is just part of the total compensation paid to that employee. It makes no difference whether it is calculated before or after it hits his or her paycheck. If the money wasn't paying for insurance, it would be part of the employee's gross wages. From the employee's perspective, it is all the employer's money. They would argue that without that insurance bill to pay, the owners would have more profit in their pockets.

In addition to the actual policy, many employees consider the convenience of employer-provided health insurance to be an intangible benefit. How easily and quickly will a medical bill be paid or reimbursed? How many pieces of paper does the employee have to touch, hold on to, or file in order to receive their benefits. With an HMO, an employee has to show a card to get services. They pay a co-payment for that visit and never see a piece of paper. Many people value this feature, but as I pointed out earlier in this chapter, this lack of information about the true costs of health services has contributed to the spiraling cost of health insurance.

The Challenge

Issues surrounding what constitutes a benefit and who's actually paying for it gets even more confusing when we put HDHPs and HSAs into the mix.

On the surface this new system for funding health care is so simple. Save a $1,050 (or more), insure the rest. No co-pays, no co-insurance (on some contracts), no drug cards (before the deductible), and if you don't use your $1,050, you get to keep it. The problem is that employees have to unlearn a very entrenched system and employers and employees both have to renegotiate this notion of whose money is really at stake. Would an employee prefer to pay a portion of the premium and watch the employer make a deposit to a savings account on their behalf? Or would the same employee prefer to have free health insurance and decide on his or her own whether to fund the savings account? Or would he or she choose to work for lower wages, and have both the insurance and the savings fully funded by the employer?

The days are gone when employees will be allowed to pretend that their health care is free. Employers will no longer be able to absorb the yearly increases in health-insurance premiums without lowering cash wages. Group health plans are at risk of being disbanded altogether in many companies, leaving many workers unable to afford or qualify for coverage on their own.

The combined strategy of HDHPs and HSAs provide a solution to the bigger problem of keeping Americans insured while it opens up new challenges that are mostly educational and administrative. In the coming chapters, I will give you tools to overcome these challenges. We have the opportunity to take back control of our health care, our health-care costs, our access to health insurance, and our future security.

The Least You Need to Know

- A qualifying High Deductible Health Plan (HDHP) is required to open a Health Savings Account (HSA).

- Those under 65 who claim themselves on their taxes may open an HSA if they are covered only by HDHPs.

- Splitting the funding of health care into the two pieces of savings and insurance makes financial sense.

- Employers will be faced with evaluating the feasibility of this strategy as traditional Health Maintenance Organizations (HMOs) and Preferred Provider Organizations (PPOs) are likely to become increasingly cost prohibitive in the near future.

Chapter 2

High Deductible
Health Plans

In This Chapter

- What makes an insurance contract an HDHP
- How HDHPs differ from the contract you now have
- Standard plan designs on the market

Sing along with me ...

"I wish I didn't know now what I didn't know then. I wish I could start this whole thing over again."

Toby Keith's sentiment in his popular country song echoes the feelings most people have when they learn about HDHPs. If you could go back to the days of innocence, way back when you knew nothing about health insurance, then I could teach you the basic concept of HDHPs in about two sentences:

- You pay for the first $1,050 of your medical expenses each year.
- The insurance company pays the rest.

But today you would respond by asking me, "What about prescriptions?" And we would dive headlong into the challenge of undoing years of programming from the insurance companies that had you convinced that health insurance had to be complicated to be good.

Treasury's Rules

The president signed Public Law 108-173 on December 8, 2003, called the "Medicare Prescription Drug, Improvement and Modernization Act of 2003." This act of Congress defined HDHPs and HSAs. Congress asked the United States Treasury Department to write rules to help taxpayers follow the law. The Internal Revenue Service (a part of the Treasury Department) will be interpreting and enforcing these rules as people file their tax returns each year.

You may have a vague notion that the Federal Government doesn't usually regulate the insurance industry. Each state has an Insurance Commissioner, who watches over the laws governing what policies can be sold in their state. But as health-insurance rates continued to skyrocket, business owners complained to their congressional representatives and the president.

The easiest way Congress can impact any consumer market is to adjust the tax code to change consumer and producer behavior. This is what they have done with HSAs. They defined which types of insurance contracts would qualify an individual to open an HSA. Insurance companies almost immediately developed qualifying products and had them approved by the state insurance commissioners for sale. The policies must have certain characteristics, which we'll go through one at a time.

High, Higher, Highest Deductible

I'm guessing you already figured out that a High Deductible Health Plan probably has to have a high deductible. But you can never be sure when the IRS is involved! And the rule could change when you're not looking. In fact, it already has.

When the first regulations were written, they stated a minimum $1,000 deductible for an individual plan and $2,000 deductible for a family plan. There is a maximum deductible requirement as well: it can be as high as $5,100 for an individual and $10,200 for a family.

Minimum deductibles are supposed to be increased by an index tied to the inflation rate, so some insurance companies started with $1,100 deductibles as the lowest deductible plans. Those that did issue $1,000 plans in 2004 pulled them off the market as 2005 approached, only to put them back when the U.S. Treasury decided not to index the minimum amount of the deductible for the 2005 plan year.

But It Looks Like a Deductible

Brace yourself. These deductibles are not really deductibles, as you have come to know and love them. If you currently have a Preferred Provider Organization (PPO) plan in place, you probably have a deductible stated in the plan benefits. I'll guess $250 or $500. What counts toward that deductible might only be services like testing out of the doctor's office, outpatient procedures, and hospitalizations. The cost of your office visits and prescriptions would be shared between a co-payment from you and the rest coming from your insurance company. But the payment for those services does not add into your deductible. You could go to the doctor once a week for a year and rack up 52 $20 co-payments equaling $1,040 and still not meet your $250 deductible.

Forget all of that. HDHP deductibles are true deductibles. Not some carved out, partially crafted notion of a deductible. If you incur an expense for a covered service, it counts toward the deductible. It has to. The rules state that you can't receive any benefit from your HDHP until *you* have met your deductible.

I Want My Co-Payments Back

There are no co-payments on these plans, which is a good thing. At first blush, employees will go through major separation anxiety. They love their co-payments. They know if Johnnie has an ear infection, it only takes $20 to see the doctor and $15 for the pink stuff. They can do that out of any week's paycheck, so they don't have to save for or go into debt for a sick kid.

Thinking about it a little further, getting rid of co-payments usually means a bonus to employees, especially those who pay a lot of co-payments. Remember that under current PPO contracts, co-payments are lost money, never counting toward a deductible, rarely being tax deductible without a *Section 125* plan and potentially never ending. With HDHPs, those expenses can now end as soon as an employee meets his or her deductible and the insurance company begins payments for those services.

Word Doctor

The Internal Revenue Service Code **Section 125** allows employers to treat certain withholdings for employee benefits as not taxable. It also allows the creation of a Flexible Spending Account that employees can use to pay for co-payments with pre-tax dollars.

Insurance Insights _____

Assuming that your mother is no longer around to tell you to go get a check-up, the rules allow for insurance companies to pay for preventive services prior to the deductible being met. You knew they couldn't have a rule without an exception, so this seemed like a good one.

Mommy, What's a Network?

Every parent should have "The Talk" with their kids as soon as they are mature enough to handle it, but young enough that they still have time to make good decisions in their lives. I mean about choosing the right network, of course. A network is a list of medical providers (doctors, hospitals, labs, pharmacies, etc.) that have signed a contract with an insurance company to provide their services at an agreed upon rate.

The Doctor's Dilemma

We know that "in network" (or on the list) is a good thing and "out of network" (not on the list) is a bad thing. But how does this happen? Every doctor could be in every network, so why aren't they? Could it be that they don't want to offer their services for 50¢ on the dollar? Could it be that they are so busy that their golf game is already suffering and

more patients would mean total disgrace on the course? Or could it be that a particular insurance company takes two months to pay their bills and the doctors would like their money faster? These are all very good reasons for a doctor not to join a network.

I'm going to assume that you like your doctor, or you wouldn't still be going to see her. Let's say she charges $75 for an established patient office visit. You are allowed to walk in the door and give her $75. You may even think that the service you just received was actually worth $75. But, wait! Don't do that! She signed a contract with your insurance company that says she is obligated to provide that service for $49. You give her the $20 copayment and she gets $29 from the insurance company. When you get your Explanations of Benefits (EOB) from the insurance company, it indicates that she reduced her fee by $26 ($75–49) to comply with the network contract. As much as you like her, you feel no guilt that you just stiffed her, right? She chose to sign that contract.

If she were not in the network, you would have been billed $75 and required to pay $75. So doing business with network providers is just like going to vendors that honor a particular discount card. And to complicate it, the charges that you incur at providers that are not in the network add up to a separate "out-of-network" deductible under your plan. The insurance companies are obviously encouraging you to "just say no" to out-of-network providers.

The Hidden Benefit

The insurance companies go to a lot of effort to build and manage their networks. It's so much work that sometimes they don't build their own, but instead lease them from managed care networks and other insurance companies. Some national insurance companies allow you to pick from several local networks. With HMOs and PPOs you cared about which doctors were in the network. If your kids' doctor wasn't in-network, you didn't buy the plan. If he was, you didn't spend a moment worrying about how much he would actually be paid by the insurance company. That was his problem.

Now you care. With an HDHP, you will be paying that network rate until your deductible is met. One network may give you $26 off of a $75 office visit, and another may only give you a $10 discount. This is such a problem right now because the networks won't disclose their negotiated rates and the doctors aren't much happier about sharing them.

Let's ignore the challenge of knowing how much of a discount there will be, and delight for a moment that there will be a discount of some amount. Remember that the law states you cannot have any benefits paid from the insurance company before you meet your deductible. It seems to me that they missed this one, or they don't see it as a benefit that your insurance company has strong-armed your doctor into taking less money for providing you services. It seems like a benefit to me. But maybe because it comes out of the doctor's or hospital's pocket, it doesn't count.

Insurance Insights

Imagine yourself standing at a sub shop deciding which of two scratch-off coupons to use but you can't scratch it off until after you order. You have no idea how much of a discount you will get until you are a customer. This is the big gap in the consumer-driven health-care movement. Call us picky, but we're used to seeing the prices before we buy. Congress has been debating what to do about this and we should see some changes in the near future.

Take It to the Limit

We used to have stop losses—sounds like a good insurance industry term, doesn't it? A stop loss was the point at which you (the insured) stopped losing money and the insurance company picked up the bill at 100 percent. Now we call them Out-of-Pocket-Limits (or maximums) and calculate them a little differently. The HDHP rules require that these limits be no greater than $5,250 for an individual and $10,500 for a family. These limits include the in-network deductible stated in your policy. However, each time you go to an out-of-network provider, those fees will add up to have stop losses into a separate deductible and Out-of-Pocket Limit.

The Plans You Know and Love

You start by meeting your deductible, the part of your expenses when you are responsible for 100 percent of the network negotiated charges. Then you have a *co-insurance* zone where you split the charges with the insurance company. Common splits are 10 percent you, 90 percent insurance company; 20 percent you, 80 percent insurance company; and 50 percent you, 50 percent insurance company. This goes on until you have spent your Out-of-Pocket Limit.

Word Doctor

Co-insurance is the term given to the range of expenses where you pay a portion and the insurance company pays a portion. It is stated as a percentage, usually 80/20 co-insurance rate, or 50/50 co-insurance rate.

Let's consider an example: Your teenager leaves his shoes at the top of the stairs. You forget that it is your job to pick them up and you trip, falling down the stairs and breaking your leg. You need surgery. The total bill is $12,000. You have an insurance plan with a $500 deductible, 80/20 percent co-insurance rate, and an Out-of-Pocket Limit of $2,000. Here's the breakdown:

	Expenses	Your Responsibility	Insurance Co. Payments
Deductible	First $500	$500	$0
Co-Insurance	Next $10,000	$2,000	$8,000
Limit Is Met	Final $1,500	$0	$1,500

The industry has not standardized the definition of Out-of-Pocket Limits, however. Some plans include the deductible in this calculation, as well. In the preceding example, that would mean a $2,500 limit. This is a very important number to you and your employees, so it's essential that you make sure you are looking at the same calculation when you compare plans.

The Co-Payments Never End

The deductibles and Out-of-Pocket Limits start over again each calendar year for most plans. If you have a plan with co-payments, you effectively have no limit to the amount you can spend in any calendar year. All the doctor visits and prescriptions you fill will have co-payments, and those expenses never add into the deductible or the Out-of-Pocket Limit.

Let's consider an example of someone with a serious ongoing illness like heart disease. As you can

see, these co-payments could add up to thousands
of dollars:

1 generic prescription/mo ($15 × 12)	$180
2 brand name prescriptions/mo ($25 × 24)	$600
1 brand new prescription/mo ($40 × 12)	$480
1 primary physician visit/mo ($20 × 12)	$240
4 specialist visits/yr ($30 × 4)	$120
2 emergency room visits/yr ($150 × 2)	$300
Total	$1,920

Our cardiac patient has reached $1,920 of expenses
and we haven't begun to calculate the deductible or
co-insurance expenses should he need any outpatient procedures or hospitalizations. Let's say that
he does end up in the hospital once during the year
and meets his Out-of-Pocket Limit. On the $500,
80/20 percent to $2,000 plan we used earlier, he
would have another $2,500 going out for a total of
$4,420 for the year.

The HDHP Calculations

Let's recalculate the preceding example using an
HDHP plan with a $2,000 deductible and 80/20
percent co-insurance with a $4,000 Out-of-Pocket
Limit (including the $2,000 deductible):

1 generic prescription/mo ($22 × 12)	$264
2 brand name prescriptions/mo ($90 × 24)	$2,160
1 brand new prescription/mo ($220 × 12)	$2,640
1 primary physician visit/mo ($50 × 12)	$600
4 specialist visits/yr ($200 × 4)	$800
2 emergency room visits/yr ($750 × 2)	= $1,500
Total	$7,960

	Expenses	Your Responsibility	Insurance Co. Payments
Deductible	First $2,000	$2,000	$0
Co-Insurance	Next $5,960	$1,192	$4,768
Limit Is Not Met			
Total		$3,192	$4,768

His current expenses total $3,192 and he would continue to pay at the 20 percent rate until he reaches the $4,000 Out-of-Pocket Limit. With one hospitalization, he would fly past this limit. Adding the $30,000 hospitalization, we're at $37,960. How much does he pay?

	Expenses	Your Responsibility	Insurance Co. Payments
Deductible	First $2,000	$2,000	$0
Co-Insurance	Next $10,000	$2,000	$8,000
Limit Is Met	Final $25,960	$0	$25,960
Total		$4,000	$33,960

His total is $4,000 and now capped at $4,000. No more co-payments to continue to run up his health-care costs for the year. But the best part is that the insurance company has funded part of this $4,000 in the form of reduced premiums when he went from the $500 deductible PPO to the $2,000 deductible HDHP. Exactly how much savings would depend on his location, age, size of his company, and so many other factors it is impossible to guess. It could range from 10 to 30 percent. This calculation will become a very important factor in deciding to move from a PPO to an HDHP. Most employers look for a significant portion of the deductible increase to be returned to them in premium savings.

Plan Possibilities

The U.S. Treasury Department issued rule after rule during 2004 and into 2005. Some companies jumped into the game anticipating what type of contract would pass the HDHP test, only to find themselves revising plan documents all year long. Others decided to wait out the initial confusion and begin selling plans later in the year. One of the largest national companies waited until January 1, 2005, which then caused market repositioning. Competitive companies are constantly revising plans to keep up with the industry leaders as well as the Treasury rule revisions.

When the Deductible Equals the Out-of-Pocket Limit

The HDHP rules allow for plans such as those I used in the preceding examples. A high deductible, followed by a co-insurance rate applied to expenses up to an Out-of-Pocket Limit. But remember my first explanation at the top of the chapter:

- You pay for the first $1,050 of your medical expenses each year.
- The insurance company pays the rest.

This basic plan design leaves out the co-insurance portion altogether. It is also allowed by the HDHP rules. These plans are known as 100 percent plans. After the deductible is paid, the insurance company begins paying 100 percent of costs. This is a very popular plan design—so much so that some insurance companies are only offering 100 percent plans. However, they are a little more expensive than plans that have a co-insurance provision.

Insurance brokers and employers are finding 100 percent plans much easier to explain to employees. In many plans currently in force, an employee might have a $250 deductible 80 percent plan with a $1,500 Out-of-Pocket Limit. The switch to a $1,000 deductible HDHP 100 percent plan would actually give the employees less potential risk. Even though their deductibles went up from $250 to $1,100 (the number they hear first), their Out-of-Pocket Limit actually went down from $1,500 to $1,100. Beyond that they have no copayments to budget for and they may end up the year with money in a bank account in their name.

Even though the deductible has risen by $850, the Out-of-Pocket Limit is $400 less. The employee actually has more insurance now than before, meaning they are accepting less risk for themselves and pooling more with the insurance company. This would be considered the "Cadillac" of HDHPs on the market and probably wouldn't realize much, if any, premium savings for the company initially. But as a starter plan, it can move employees to the new concept while actually giving them better coverage.

To Embed or Not to Embed

All the examples I have used so far involve a person with single coverage. When we bring family coverage into the conversation we need to learn a new term: *embedded deductible*. Don't look now, but you've got one if you have family coverage on a PPO plan. You're used to it even though you probably didn't know it had a name. Let's say your plan has a $250 per person deductible and you need to meet it two times for your family. After you've met the per person deductible twice, the other 10 kids get a pass. We might state that your plan has a $500 family deductible, but it doesn't. It has two $250 embedded deductibles.

When HDHPs were introduced to the market in 2004, they didn't have embedded deductibles. If the plan stated a $1,000 individual/$2,000 family deductible it meant that the family had to reach $2,000 before insurance benefits would start. It did not mean that two people had to meet a $1,000 deductible each. You could get to the $2,000 any way you like. Each of your ten kids could have a $200 doctor visit, or your poor, tired, wife could be hospitalized for exhaustion and easily meet the deductible all by herself.

Then someone posed the question, "What if the individual deductible is $2,000? Since that meets the minimum family deductible stated in the law, can't we embed deductibles after that amount?" It took the U.S. Treasury some time to think about that one, but they eventually said, "Sure, why not?"

So it got complicated again. Some companies antic-
ipated this decision and are now only offering plans
with embedded deductibles. Other companies are
still only offering nonembedded deductibles and
considering changing future plan offerings.

Embedded deductibles have value to employees
with family coverage. You'll pay more for plans
that offer this feature. If your group has a lot of
employees electing family coverage, they will benefit from these deductibles. If everyone working for
your company is single, you'd be able to consider
plans without embedded deductibles at a lower
cost.

Withdrawal Pains

Going cold turkey off of co-payments, prescription
benefits, and preventive care seemed like too much
for some people to handle, so the U.S. Treasury
allowed a phase-in period, which was over January
1, 2006. Until then some plans offered some drug
benefits before the deductible.

Many plans are requiring a drug co-payment after
the deductible as a standard feature. Because of
what I'll call "co-payment confusion," I've watched
employees sigh a big sigh of relief that they can
have their co-payments again. Do the math! This is
not a good thing. This means more money out of
the employee's pocket.

Let's assume they have an 80/20 percent co-insurance rate and they've met their deductible. The drug card is now activated requiring them to pay $30 for a brand name drug. At 20 percent, the drug would have to cost over $150 in order for the $30 to be a better cost.

Co-payments are the hair of the dog that bit us. By shielding us from the true cost of our health care, we have arrived at a predictable point where we are consuming more than we value. It is no surprise that we have grown attached to them and would want them to continue. As you shop for HDHPs be careful of the notion that co-payments after the deductible are a good thing for employees. They actually work to shift more costs to the employees who are using the most health-care services, and thereby keep premiums lower.

The healthy replacement for co-payments is a well-funded Health Savings Account. In the next chapter, we will explore those contracts and look for more ways to keep costs at a minimum while enhancing your employees' financial security.

The Least You Need to Know

- High Deductible Health Plans have a minimum $1,050 and maximum $5,250 deductible for individuals, $2,100 and $10,500 limits for families.
- Out-of-Pocket Limits are $5,250 for individuals and $10,500 for families.

- All medical expenses count toward the deductible and are paid for at the network negotiated rate with in-network providers.

- The plans do not have co-payments or other benefits, except preventive care, prior to the deductible. Some plans have prescription co-payments after the deductible.

Chapter

Health Savings Accounts

In This Chapter

- What makes a Savings Account a Health Savings Account
- Who can open an account
- The rules regarding deposits and withdrawals

I've been told I have a slightly strange definition of what qualifies as entertainment. Recently, I picked a main street in our town with a row of branch banks. Just for fun, I walked into each asking about their Health Savings Accounts. The responses ranged from, "We have lots of savings accounts here," to, "I've never heard of that," to, "I think we're supposed to have them soon, can you come back in a little while?"

With as much confusion as there has been in the health insurance side of this new strategy, there has been even more confusion on the savings side. The regional banks were very slow to come to market with these products and very secretive about why it took so long. It would seem that they haven't really decided that these accounts will be profitable. It may take a while for these banks to find their niche in this market.

The national banks and investment firms are finding a market by teaming up with the insurance companies to sell the two contracts (insurance and savings) as a package. These alliances are taking several forms. Some insurance companies have purchased banks so they can control the marketing of the accounts. Some have endorsed a specific account provider by training their insurance sales force to open those accounts. Others are co-branding marketing material.

Why Call It a Savings Account?

Back in those innocent days when health insurance was simple, bank accounts were simple, too. Savings accounts were identified with cute little passbooks you took to the bank to have the teller write in the amounts you deposited and withdrew. Checking accounts had, you guessed it, checkbooks. Then one day we discovered NOW (Negotiable Order of Withdrawal) accounts and we lost our innocence. These accounts combined the convenience of a checking account with the interest-bearing feature of a savings account. Ever since then it has been a little hard to tell them apart.

It's the Tax Status

I hate to be the one to break it to you but a Health Savings Account is not really a type of account. It is a tax status given to any number of places you can park your cash. Just like Individual Retirement Accounts, the status can be attached to a variety of banking and investment instruments. So an account at one bank, labeled as an HSA, may have very different provisions than an account at the next bank. They will both have the same tax treatment, however.

A bank could sell you what looks and acts just like a checking account … but wait! It *is* a checking account, even though they can call it a Health Savings Account once it qualifies for the preferential tax status. An investment company could sell you a mutual fund account and call it a Health Savings Account. Some banks offer CDs that qualify. Other investment firms offer money market funds. The market is still figuring out what type of financial vehicles people will want to use for these funds.

Helping Out Medicare

Congress named these accounts all Health Savings Accounts with the hope that the not-too-subtle hint that you should *save* something wouldn't be lost on you. As much as they are aware that you have had it with high health-insurance costs, they are equally afraid of how mad you will be if Medicare isn't there for you when you retire. The birth of HSAs was a part of the Medicare Act, after all. The tax break that your employees get on their Medicare tax (part of FICA) is a tiny way to privatize a piece of the Medicare system. The hope is that if a percentage of the population is given an incentive to save for a portion of their medical expenses in retirement, Medicare may have a lightened load.

Insurance Insights _____

Medicare currently covers about 36 million elderly and 7 million people under 65 with permanent disabilities. The total is projected to reach 72 million by 2025, when the last of the baby boomers reach age 65.

The term *savings* does not apply to everyone, however. If you have a chronic illness, you may open a checking account that qualifies as a Health Savings Account, place the maximum deposit in it each year, and spend it immediately. You won't ever *save* a penny, but it's still a Health Savings Account. If you do have the opportunity to save, it is a marvelous financial vehicle for accumulating tax-free savings. We'll talk about a variety of strategies in Chapter 10.

Who Can Have an Account

It isn't very hard to qualify for an HSA. Congress wrote the requirements to include potentially almost all working Americans. We learned in Chapter 2 that the person must be covered by at least one High Deductible Health Plan (HDHP). They cannot be covered by any private health insurance or public insurance program (such as Medicare or Medicaid) that is not an HDHP. They must be under 65 years old, and no one else may have the right to claim them on their tax return.

Most employees have the potential to qualify. Persons who would be excluded are those over 65, those eligible to be claimed by someone else for tax purposes, and those covered by public insurance programs. A big stumbling block for many workers is that they are covered by both their employer's plan, which is an HDHP, and their spouse's plan, which is not an HDHP. This non-HDHP coverage disqualifies them to open or contribute to an HSA. But the second they drop the non-HDHP coverage they become eligible.

 HSA Hazards

You must have an HDHP in place to qualify for an HSA, but the reverse is not true. You do not have to open an HSA when you purchase an HDHP. If you are installing a group HDHP and covering some workers who are ineligible for an HSA, they are still eligible to be covered by the HDHP.

Ownership and Responsibility

Here's the hardest part for you to get out of your system. You have become accustomed to the notion that tax deferred funds you deposit on behalf of your employees become your problem, in some way. But with these accounts, once the money is in the account, titled to the employee, all responsibilities fall to them. You, as the employer, have no ownership, responsibility, or control of these accounts. You do not have a fiduciary responsibility over them.

If you are contributing to the accounts, you do have an obligation to make those contributions fairly across all your covered employees. What constitutes fairness is not difficult. We will discuss how to comply in the next chapter. You can also decide that your contribution will go to one designated financial institution, eliminating the headache of dozens of checks you must write per month to deposit to the employees' accounts.

 HSA Hazards

> The bank, investment company, or insurance company that opens your HSA is referred to as the *trustee* of your account. They have guidelines and tax reporting responsibilities to follow. They are not, however, required to verify that you are covered by a qualified HDHP. That is up to you.

Once the money is in the account, the employee is responsible for managing it according to the tax laws. If they choose to withdraw the money for a trip to the Caribbean, they are likely to be taxed and penalized by the IRS for that withdrawal. It is no different than any other deduction they claim. They must save the supporting documentation and, if audited, present it to the IRS.

Along with that responsibility comes the freedom to move (roll over) the money to any trustee they choose. They can have as many accounts open at the same time as they have the ability to manage. The only limitation is that the total deposits to all accounts cannot exceed their yearly maximum, which is explained in the next section.

Regardless of who makes the deposit, as soon as it shows in the balance of the account, it is the employee's money. If the employee quits, the money continues to be the employee's money. Nothing changes. It's important for employers to take this fact into account when determining when to deposit money into employee's accounts. We will discuss timing issues in Chapter 8.

The Ins and Outs

Getting money in and out of HSAs seems to be the most anxiety-producing financial task since people started using their credit cards to make online purchases. Since HSA deposits and withdrawals can be taxed and penalized, it may feel like you're never sure if you really did it right. The IRS creates rules and regulations that most of us never see. We'll go into more depth on these rules in the next chapter, but let's start by looking at how much we can put in and take out and who can do it.

Maximum Deposits

During 2006, a person with individual coverage from an HDHP can put in up to $2,700, with two catches: They must have the coverage in place for the entire calendar year (not insurance plan year) and the deductible on their HDHP has to be at least $2,700.

If their plan started after January 1, 2006, the amount they can contribute would be reduced by $1/12$ for each month they weren't covered.

Example: You offer your employees a choice of plans each year on the renewal of your company's health plan, April 1. This year (2006) you include a $3,000 deductible HDHP option, which Brittany selects. Since three months (or $3/12$ of the year) has passed, she can only deposit $9/12$ of $2,700 or $2,025, during 2006.

In this example, Brittany would be able to make the deposit to her HSA anytime between April 1, 2006, the start date of her HDHP coverage and April 15, 2007, the deadline for making deposits for the 2006 tax year. She can do it in one lump sum, divide it over her paydays, or choose any other timing that works for her.

If the plan you select has a deductible of less than
$2,700, then the yearly deposit is limited to that
amount and adjusted for the number of months
covered.

Example: You offer your employees an HDHP
with a $2,000 deductible that begins at your
renewal date, April 1, 2006. The total yearly
deposit allowed of $2,000 is prorated for 2005.
Since there are 9 months left in the year, each
employee can deposit $9/12$ of $2,000 or $1,500.

The same calculation holds if an employee cancels
an HDHP sometime during the year.

Example: Jason was working for you on January 1,
2005, and decided to deposit the full HDHP
deductible of $2,400 for the year into his HSA
account during January. He quits July 1, 2006 and
goes to work for an employer who does not offer
an HDHP. He must withdraw and pay taxes on
$1,200, representing $6/12$ of $2,400.

A similar calculation would be made if employees
change the deductible on their HDHPs during the
year. They would need to increase or decrease,
accordingly, to match the deductible. To make it
simple, I think about this formula as being
monthly: each month you earn the right to deposit
$1/12$ of your plan's current deductible (not to exceed
the IRS maximum of $220). You are not required
to deposit that amount, nor restricted from
depositing the allowed amount in advance of earning the right.

Family Coverage Deposits

If your employee chooses family coverage on his HDHP, then the HSA deposit limit increases. The maximum deposit for 2006 is $5,450. Each HDHP plan will have a family deductible that is usually twice the individual deductible. Family coverage is defined as Employee/Spouse, Employee/Child(ren), and Employee/Spouse/Child(ren). By electing any of these coverage options, the employee qualifies to put the family deductible, up to the IRS maximum, into their HSA account.

HSA accounts are always individual accounts, however. Even though two spouses may be covered by the HDHP, only the wife, who works for you, would be named as an owner of the account. If her husband is covered by an HDHP at his employer and chooses family coverage, he can also open an HSA. The family contribution would be split between the two of them and limited to the lower of the two deductibles on their respective plans.

Catch Up Deposits

Between the ages of 55 and 64, an individual can make a catch-up contribution each year. This amount began as $500 in 2004 and will increase $100 per year until it reaches $1,000 for the 2009 tax year. This amount is per person, not per account. So if an employee has family coverage and both he and his wife are 57 years old, in 2006 they can deposit a total of $1,400 over the maximum using the calculations we just learned. The catch-up contributions are also prorated for how many months during the year the account is open.

Who Can Make the Deposits

Anyone can make a deposit into anyone else's HSA account. Only the owner of the account will get the tax deduction for the deposit, however. Likewise, the owner of the account will be penalized if too much is deposited.

It is very common for employers to make deposits on behalf of their employees. The employer can then take the deposit as a business deduction. This avoids both sides of the FICA contribution (employer and employee) as well. I'll walk you through the tax strategies in more detail in the next chapter.

Insurance Insights

The Internal Revenue Service Code Section 125 allows employees to use pre-tax income to pay for insurance premiums. If an employer does not have a Section 125 plan, the employees' contributions would be made using after-tax dollars and then adjusted to reduce their taxable income on their 1040 filing.

Most of the time the individual is making at least some of the deposits themselves. These deposits are divided into two categories, pre-tax and post-tax. The pre-tax contributions would be made through their employer's cafeteria (Section 125) plan as a payroll deduction. The post-tax contributions could also be made through a payroll deduction or just directly out of their net paycheck. Both contributions will be ultimately deductible from gross wages for income tax purposes. The pre-tax contributions will avoid FICA tax as well.

Getting Money Out

The money in an HSA can be withdrawn at any time for any reason. And you thought the money was just for health expenses. There is no law that prevents you from spending it whenever and wherever you wish. There is only a tax incentive to spend it on an approved list of medical expenses and insurance premiums. If you pick something from the list (Appendix B) the money will not be taxed. If you pick something not on the list, the money will be taxed. If you are under 65 and not disabled, the money will also be subject to a 10 percent penalty (excise tax).

 HSA Hazards

Be aware that the list of qualified medical expenses and insurance premiums includes items that do not qualify for the deductible on the HDHP (e.g. dental expenses). This can create some confusion that employees will need to sort out in order to manage their HSAs effectively.

There are two attitudes an employer can have about this feature of the accounts. The first is to not spend one second worrying that the employee may spend it on something other than approved, tax-free expenses. The employer has no liability, no fiduciary responsibility, and no obligation to pay the employee's tax penalties. They know that some people in the world are just financially reckless and occasionally they come to work for them.

The second attitude is to worry, or care, or even get angry that the money may be used for non-medical expenses. This usually happens when it is "employer's money" that is being used to fund the account. These employers take a more parental role with their employees and are truly trying to enhance their financial security by providing benefits. You need to decide which kind of employer you are in order to design the best strategy for funding the accounts. Keep this in mind as you select a plan design.

The Least You Need to Know

- The term "Health Savings Account" refers to the preferred tax status given to a variety of financial vehicles.
- The accounts can be funded by employees, employers, and others, with a deduction from gross income enjoyed by the employee, up to the calendar year maximum allowed by the IRS.

- The accounts are titled to an individual and are completely portable between trustees. The employer has no fiduciary responsibility over the accounts.

- Money in the accounts becomes tax deferred and withdrawals are tax-free if used for a medical expense or insurance premium on the IRS's approved list.

Chapter 4

Taxes, Taxes, and Less Taxes

In This Chapter

- The tax treatment of HSAs
- The IRS forms you will need
- The record keeping required

Taxes seem to be the tail wagging the dog of our health-care system. Congress wagged them enough that we sat up and begged for a new system of health insurance. We love our tax treats and the notion that something is now cheaper because we aren't paying taxes on the money we use to buy it. We also love to watch our real returns on our investments increase because they aren't being taxed.

When Congress was debating the provisions of the Medicare bill some people wanted to include vitamins and supplements on the list of items you could buy with tax-free HSA withdrawals. Sounds like a reasonable notion to me. If you keep people healthier, they may not need as much health care. But the provision was shot down because it was too expensive. How could that be? When Congress adds up the cost of a tax cut, it considers the cost to the federal budget. By adding more items to the list, taxpayers would potentially take more deductions and pay fewer taxes. That takes money out of the hands of the federal government. Unless they cut an expense somewhere else, they'd have to raise your taxes on other items to make up for it.

Insurance Insights

UnitedHealthcare and their subsidiary, Golden Rule, reported that by mid-2005, 18 percent of those covered by their HDHPs and HSAs did not previously have health-insurance coverage. Assurant Health reported in February 2005 that 40 percent of their HDHP applicants listed no prior coverage.

So they compromised with a tax cut that they felt would be affordable and at the same time encourage people to use health-insurance strategies that are in the best interest of the economy and national health-care policy. They knew that the decision to move to the new products would be made primarily by small business owners. Therefore, it had to make sense for their family's financial security before they could consider it for the rest of the company.

What Does It Mean to You?

If you are a successful business owner with a family and you purchase an HDHP that allows you the maximum contribution to an HSA each year, your tax savings will be a minimum of $1,500 per year. To that amount we can add FICA savings of $800 (if you are also an employee of your company) and possibly state and local income tax savings. This means that more than 40 percent of the deposit to your HSA will be funded by the federal government through your tax savings. It's possible that the other 60 percent would come from savings on your insurance premiums. You may end up with a savings account that costs you nothing more than you are already spending.

HSAs are being added to the list of why a business owner would want to form a corporation. Like other tax issues, there is an advantage to being an employee of your company, instead of an owner/partner. Let's look at how the taxes are calculated in a variety of ownership situations.

Owners and Partners

If you are an owner of a business, your company's profits flow through to your personal income tax return. As an owner, you will use a Schedule C to calculate the profit or loss. You carry forward this number to your Form 1040, line 12. This profit plus any other income you had adds up to your total income.

You then make adjustments to your total income at the bottom of the front page of the 1040. A new line 25 in that section is labeled "Health savings account deduction. Attach Form 8889." This is where you enter the amount from line 11 on Form 8889. Form 8889 is a universal form that is now required for anyone making deposits into or taking withdrawals out of an HSA.

Once you calculate your Adjusted Gross Income, you calculate your deductions and arrive at your Taxable Income. Because the HSA contribution is an adjustment to income, it doesn't matter if you itemize your deductions or take the standard deduction. The HSA contribution reduces your taxable income dollar for dollar, and therefore reduces the tax you pay.

Let's go back to the Schedule C for a minute. You also take your profit or loss from your business and carry it over to the Schedule SE to calculate your Self-Employment Tax, a.k.a Social Security or FICA tax. Your HSA contribution will not affect this calculation since it does not reduce your income until you arrive at the 1040 calculations. So making a contribution to an HSA will not reduce your Social Security or Medicare taxes.

If you are a partner in a business, you will receive similar treatment for income taxes and FICA taxes. Your income is reported to you by the partnership on a K-1 form. The net income or loss from the K-1 is carried to the 1040 on line 17. The adjustment to income for the HSA contribution on line

25 will reduce this income for tax purposes. Your contribution, as well, will not affect the calculation for FICA taxes.

Premium Advice

In many businesses, the HSA contributions are made by the business on behalf of all the employees. If the business makes a contribution on behalf of partners, this contribution needs to be added back into the amount reported on the K-1.

You Employ Yourself

If your corporation hires you to work for it, you qualify for the same tax treatment that is afforded all your other employees. If you take money that has already been taxed through your payroll calculations and deposit it into an HSA, you can adjust your income on Form 1040, line 25. You will have to complete Form 8889 as well. So your final income tax calculation for the year will factor in the HSA contribution.

Since you are using after tax dollars to make the deposit, the FICA tax has already been withheld. The employer portion of the FICA tax has also been paid. You will not be able to recover this tax through your year-end tax filing.

If you would like to avoid paying FICA tax on HSA deposits you have two options, which I'll cover in the following section regarding all your employees.

What Does It Mean to Your Employees?

Now it gets interesting and a little confusing, due to all the options you have. We will discuss strategies for which options work best for your company in Chapter 7. For the moment, let's just plow through what options there are.

The Employees Make the Deposit Themselves

Just as owners, partners, and employed stockholders may do, the rank and file employees may take money from their after-tax net paychecks and make a deposit into an HSA account. Your payroll would not usually be involved, unless the employee has asked for a direct deposit to that account. Your payroll service would send this money electronically and may not be aware that this account number is an HSA.

The employee is responsible for determining the appropriate amount to deposit so as not to exceed the annual maximum allowed by the IRS. The employee takes the deduction on their tax return at the end of the year. This is one of the stumbling blocks for many employees. They will not be able to adjust their income for an HSA contribution without filing the 1040 long form—they cannot use the 1040A or 1040EZ short forms. For many who pay a tax service to complete and file their returns, there will be an additional cost to prepare the 8889 and the 1040. For those who complete their forms themselves, it will require additional time and education to learn about the longer form. Tax preparation software will no doubt include the schedule 8889 and generate the longer form automatically.

The Employer Makes the Deposits for the Employees

As the employer, you are allowed to deposit money into HSA accounts on behalf of employees and claim the deposit as an employee benefit business expense. The amount you deposit is not included in the employee's gross income for calculating the employee's federal income tax, Social Security, or Medicare tax. It is also excluded from the calculation of the employer's Social Security, Medicare, and Federal Unemployment tax. This amount is, however, reported on the W-2 in box 12 with a code of 'W.'

The Employer Withholds the Deposits Through a Section 125 Plan

Section 125 Plans (also called Cafeteria Plans) have been around for quite some time and allow pre-tax withholding from employees' paychecks for a variety of employee benefits. The most common plans are called POP or Premium-Only Plans. This is a simple election that allows the premiums that employees pay toward the company's group insurance plans to be withheld before taxes are calculated.

If you are one of the few companies left that has not needed one of these plans, it will take very little effort from your payroll service, accountant, insurance agent or third-party administrator to help you get one going. If you already have one in place, you can amend it to allow you to treat HSA withholdings the same as premium withholdings. If you have a Section 125 and also use it to allow contributions to a Flexible Spending Account (FSA) we will discuss how that plan interacts with an HSA in Chapter 11.

Once the Section 125 document is amended to allow for HSA contributions, employees can elect a voluntary withholding from their paycheck that you would then deposit on their behalf into their account. The amount they elect would be excludable from income and therefore, not be subject to federal income tax, FICA and FUTA tax. Your payroll service will likely be able to make these deposits for you, just as they might deposit tax withholdings and net paychecks electronically.

 HSA Hazards

If your state or local government imposes an income tax, you will need to consult with a local accountant on the tax treatment of HSA contributions. Assume they are taxable until you learn otherwise.

Form 5498-SA

The trustee holding the HSA money will send each account holder a Form 5498-SA by May 31 following each tax year. This form indicates the amount of money contributed to the HSA for that tax year. It also indicates any money rolled over from an existing HSA account to this account. Because this form arrives after the filing deadline of the 1040, the account holder does not have to submit it with his or her tax return. It is a good way to double check the contribution amount reported on the 8889, though. The IRS will no doubt be matching up these amounts to look for discrepancies.

Getting the Money Out Tax-Free

As stated previously, it is up to the account holders to manage their own withdrawals. It is neither the job of the employer, the trustee, nor the IRS to let the account holders know that they have spent the money incorrectly.

The ownership of an HSA adds a new level of complexity to a person's financial life. Account holders must keep detailed records of their expenditures to prove to the IRS that they followed the rules. Even the notion of tracking their HSA account balance to know what there is to spend in the account may be new to people who are used to operating strictly with cash. Education may be the key for those employer groups who employ younger or less educated workforces that have not yet developed these skills.

Premium Advice _____

Each of the new tax forms developed to service HSA accounts are included in Appendix B. The 8889 is the most important one to become familiar with, as it is the one you will actually have to fill out and file.

Withdrawal Choices

Most HSA accounts come with debit cards. In fact, some only come with debit cards. If you use a debit card at the pharmacy counter at your grocery store, it will be reflected on your bank statement and look something like this:

3/5/06 SaveMore Pharmacy $46.78

You can save the receipt from that shopping trip and keep it with the statement if you want more proof. You can do the same thing at doctors' offices, testing labs, and hospitals—most will accept a debit card.

If you prefer checks, you can write the check to your health-care provider. For record-keeping purposes, it's a good idea to attach the receipt to the cancelled check.

You can also write yourself a check to reimburse yourself for an item you may have put on your credit card (for the cash-back feature). Or you can withdraw cash at an automated teller machine and pay the provider or yourself in cash. These transactions would most definitely need receipts to support the deduction.

Form 1099-SA

Each year the account holder will receive a 1099-SA (stands for Savings Account) from the trustee of the HSA. The trustee uses this form to report to the IRS the total of the withdrawals from the HSA. The trustee is also required to send a copy of the statement to the account holder.

The account holder will report on the 8889 the amount of the qualified medical expenses that they withdrew from the account during the tax year. The IRS does not require you to file the back-up documentation (receipts, statements, etc.), but you should store these documents with your tax information in case of a future tax audit.

Since no one is really supervising the account, the account holder can withdraw the money for any reason. The 1099-SA totals all money withdrawn, not just the qualified medical expenses. So the difference between the amount on the 1099-SA and the amount of qualified medical expenses is calculated on the 8889. If the account holder used money to pay for nonqualified expenses, this amount is reported on line 21 of Form 1040. The additional 10 percent excise tax on these withdrawals is added into line 60 on Form 1040.

The Return of Record Keeping

With HMOs, the big advance in health care for most people was the lack of headaches associated with filing and tracking all the claims. By the time you saw a piece of paper, if ever, the claim was already adjudicated and paid. That has all changed with HSAs, where we must once again keep detailed records. But don't worry, it's really quite easy to get the documentation you need to prove to the IRS that you're spending the money on approved items and services.

If you use an HSA to pay the medical expenses that fall into the high deductible of your health plan, you may swipe a debit card or write a check. Later you may get a bank statement indicating a payment to that provider. This is your record that the withdrawal from the account was for a qualified medical expense. As long as you keep it (hence the term, record-keeping) you will be fine when the tax auditor comes to call.

Sometimes it makes more sense to pay for an expense with another account, such as a credit card that earns you bonus points. The IRS allows you to reimburse yourself for these expenses or pay the credit card bill with the HSA. The record keeping for these transactions will be more difficult. You will probably have to establish a paper trail that clearly shows the money is being used for qualified medical expenses.

Qualified Insurance Premiums

The premiums of some health-insurance policies are approved as qualified withdrawals in the HSA rules. Your HDHP, however, is not one of these approved expenses, at least while you are employed. This means that if you take money out of your HSA to pay your HDHP premium, you will pay taxes and the extra 10 percent excise tax on these premiums. The types of policies that do qualify are …

- *COBRA* coverage
- Other health insurance while receiving unemployment insurance benefits
- Long-term care insurance
- Medicare Part B and D coverage

Word Doctor

COBRA stands for Consolidated Omnibus Budget Reconciliation Act. This law requires employers with 20 or more employees to allow employees to remain covered by the group health-insurance policy at their own expense for 18 months after they severe employment.

Proving these expenses during an audit should be fairly easy, but don't forget to hold on to copies of supporting information with your tax records. For instance, it is likely that your Medicare Part B premiums will be withheld from your Social Security check, so you will need to reimburse yourself for this expense.

Timing of Withdrawals

Here is one of the most interesting rules in the current HSA guidelines. With all the specifics surrounding how much money you can put in during any given tax year, there is no limit or requirement regarding the withdrawal of money for qualified expenses. Those who have suffered with the "use it or lose it" system imposed by Flexible Spending Accounts find this hard to get used to.

 HSA Hazards

> Many employees, especially those who have worked at larger employers, are familiar with Flexible Spending Accounts. The employee could make the deposit to this account and get a tax break, but lose the money at the end of each year if they didn't use it. HSAs do not have a "use it or lose it" provision, but many employees may think they do.

Let's say one of your employees deposits the maximum he is allowed under your $2,000 deductible HDHP into his HSA for three years. He now has $6,500 (including interest) in his account. He has

withdrawn nothing, even though he incurred $800
of expenses for checkups and colds over those three
years (and saved his receipts.) At the end of year
three you lay him off. He elects COBRA for $250
per month. He can withdraw the $800 to reim-
burse himself for the previous years' medical
expenses and the $250 premium per month while
he is covered by COBRA. At the end of his 18
months of COBRA, he is still unemployed and his
HSA balance is $700. He can then withdraw the
funds to pay the premium on an individual health-
insurance policy. None of these withdrawals will
prompt any taxation of the funds.

Insurance Insights

HSAs are so flexible that you can leave
the money in the account and reimburse
yourself well into your retirement when you
actually need the funds to live on. So, you
won't lose the ability to get the money out
tax-free as long as you have the records to
prove the qualifying expenses.

Covered Individuals

Here's another quirky thing about the rules that
most people don't believe. This just doesn't sound
like something the IRS would allow. Let's say one
of your employees has an HDHP and opens an
HSA through you, but his wife is covered by a

PPO at her employer. Your employee can use the funds in his HSA to pay for her unreimbursed expenses, e.g. office visit co-payments and out-of-pocket costs. Remember that her insurance coverage prohibits her from contributing to her own HSA, but surprisingly it doesn't prohibit him from paying her expenses out of his HSA tax-free. Any of his dependents would enjoy the same benefit from the HSA funds.

The Least You Need to Know

- Owners and partners who are not employees receive the same income tax treatment as employees, except that FICA tax will not be waived on the contributions.

- You'll need all records to support the deductions taken on your HSA if you are ever audited.

- The employer's only reporting obligation is to reflect employer contributions to an employee's HSA on the W-2 in box 12.

- HSA funds can be withdrawn tax-free for qualified medical expenses and insurance premiums for the account holder and family members. There is no time limit on when the withdrawal must be made.

Chapter 5

Smart Shopping for HDHPs

In This Chapter

- Comparing rates when shopping for an HDHP
- Finding and evaluating insurance companies
- Considering plan features

You know the steps to this dance. The music starts when your renewal letter arrives from your current health-insurance carrier. You check one competitor and then another, looking for the best partner without stepping on your employees' toes. This time around the floor you have an extra beat to contend with—HSAs.

Bundled HDHPs and HSAs

You now understand that there are two contracts involved in using a Health Savings Account: a high deductible insurance contract (HDHP) and a savings contract (HSA). You can pick them separately or together (bundled). You can have an HDHP without an HSA, but not vice versa. You can move or change the provisions of one without affecting the other, except when calculating the HSA deposit maximum. These really are two separate contracts.

Even though you understand this completely, the market will begin to confuse you by doing things like …

- Referring to an HDHP as an HSA plan, leaving out the word "compatible."

- Selling you the two contracts together and hiding the fees for the HSA inside the premiums for the HDHP.

- Going one step further and artificially increasing the interest rate quoted on the HSA by charging a higher premium for the HDHP.

- Offering high deductible plans (saver plans) that may on the surface look like they are HSA compatible but aren't.

Companies that bundle these two contracts together offer the key selling point of seamless administration. The main argument against the bundling is that most people prefer to do business with a local bank where they can drive down the street and talk with a person when they need to.

Banks have been brokering insurance for a while. Insurance companies have been offering investment accounts that have had banking features for a while as well. So it is possible that you could walk into your bank and buy both contracts or call up your insurance agent and buy both contracts. Maybe you should do business with both and get the respective products that they have had the most experience offering the market.

My best advice is to check out all your options. As you explore these products, the market may change right in front of your eyes. Everything is still evolving to respond to consumer demands. If you have a dynamite insurance agency, you may want to bundle the two products together so you can get the ongoing service through their office. If you have a great relationship with your banker, this is another bone you can throw them to demonstrate your loyalty as a customer. Or you may want to enter into each contract with a company that has the best track record with that piece of the strategy.

As you begin to ask around, there are some basic things you'll want to know about the products. Let's learn what questions to ask and what answers to look for.

Shopping for HDHPs

Just admit it! You love buying health insurance. Renewal season is your favorite time of year. Your insurance company sends you that nice letter explaining how wonderful they are and how much they value you as a customer. And, by the way, your rates are going up 20 percent. Do they just expect you to smile and pay the bill?

Chances are you've been shopping around in the last couple of years as rates have risen ridiculously, so you know the drill. You send around your company's employee *census* data, watch the quotes come in, collect medical information to get firm rates with some carriers, and then compare the results. It's a lot of hassle.

Word Doctor

When an insurance company asks for a **census** they are looking for a list of your full-time employees. They will need birth date, gender, marital status (spouse's birth date), number of children, and coverage selected.

In the last few years before HDHPs, you were given several pretty standard options for keeping these costs under control:

- Raise overall deductibles or add deductibles on drug coverage
- Raise co-payments on office visits or drug coverage
- Raise co-insurance rates and increase out-of-pocket limits
- Require your employees to share more of the premium cost

At some point, every employer gets to the place where making these changes affects their ability to hire, motivate, and retain good workers. What began as a perk to compete for a productive work-force is now becoming a liability as employees complain. If their yearly pay raise is gobbled up by an increase in their health-insurance rates or co-payment amounts, they won't be happy.

Fact vs. Fiction

Rates aren't always what they seem. Depending upon the size of your company and the rules in your state, initial quotes from insurers will be fiction. They call it, "subject to underwriting." This means they look at the medical information or pre-vious claims experience from your employees and give you the real rate later. But even this rate may be fiction. Until you fill out a complete application, figure out exactly who will be taking which plan (if you offer more than one), and send in a check to bind the coverage, you won't know your final rates. At that point, if you don't like the rates, you might have to start over again with the carrier that came in second place.

This frustrating process becomes even more diffi-cult when you are making the significant change to HDHPs. Some employees who waived coverage in the past may now want to be on the plan and some will want off the plan. If you are easing into this option by giving employees a choice, there may be a lot of indecision. Each time someone changes their mind, the rates can change again.

Selections at Your Current Carrier

The major exception to this confusing process is the offer from your current insurance company. When they send you the renewal letter that details your rate increase, they usually include alternate plan designs to select from. The rates on these plans are firm offers from that company. There will be no additional underwriting questions or procedures if you want to change plan designs.

Each renewal letter may include 5 to 10 alternate plans to look at. Most companies now include one or two HDHP options in this letter as well. This is a great way to get a first glimpse at how these plan rates compare to your current coverage. But the chances are that you are seeing only a few of the 10 or 20 plan designs offered by your carrier. You will need to ask to see all of them in order to make an informed choice about moving to an HDHP.

Using the renewal letter as a launching point for exploring HDHP options poses one major problem. Each state's insurance department requires that this letter arrive 30 or 60 days before your contract renewal date, but the process to move from a PPO plan to an HDHP with accompanying HSAs takes as long as 90 days to do well. We will cover the entire process in Chapter 9, but for now be aware that if you wait for your renewal letter to arrive before you begin shopping, you probably won't be installing an HDHP on your renewal date—at least not with another carrier.

HSA Hazards _____

> If you choose a plan with embedded
> deductibles, the maximum contribution to
> the HSA will be the number of people in
> the family multiplied by the embedded
> deductible, up to the IRS maximum contri-
> bution for that year.

Changing to an HDHP with your current carrier
eliminates a lot of the shopping hassles. It also
makes the transition easier for employees. If the
carrier stays the same, it is likely that their doctors
will still be in the network. For a lot of employers
this is the easiest transition to make. If you add a
second option of an HDHP to your plan design
and let employees move to the new plan as they are
comfortable, it can minimize much of the anxiety.

Of course, there is no guarantee that the plan
designs offered by your current carrier will suit
your company. And there is no assurance that their
rates will be competitive. If your renewal date is
fast approaching and you're feeling pressure to
make a decision, you can change to an HDHP at
your current carrier rather easily. This will give
you another month or two to shop for comparable
plans with other carriers. Your company will guarantee your rates for a year, but you have no obligation to remain with that company for that year.

If you use this two-step approach, you can put the HSA contracts into place and leave them where they are even if you find better HDHP plans or rates elsewhere. Remember that the HSAs are separate contracts from the HDHP and much harder to move than the HDHP. When you move HSA contracts you are asking each employee to open a new checking or investment account. They would have the option of rolling over money from the old account they owned into the new account.

Age Banded vs. Composite Rates

Large employers, usually defined as those with more than 50 employees, are billed a flat premium for each employee. This is called composite rating. A 20-year-old male is charged the same amount as 50-year-old female. When the insurance company initially calculated the rates, they took into account how many males and females, youngsters and oldsters, there were in the group. They averaged these rates into one rate for every employee, and then provided a rate for employees with spouses, employees with children, and employees with families. Throughout the policy year, if the company fired all the young employees and hired only seasoned ones, the rates would not change until the next renewal offer.

Very small employers, with under 15 employees, ordinarily are not offered composite rates. They receive a chart showing the rates by age bands (e.g., 35-39, 40-44, 45-49, etc.) and gender bands.

Each person that leaves or joins their company will change the monthly billing on the policy based on these rates. If an employee changes age band (or gender) in the middle of a policy year, their rates would change accordingly.

Those employers with between 15 and 50 employees often have a choice. Ask each insurer that quotes HDHPs for you if they can give you this type of billing. It might make the change to HDHPs much easier and even out the costs of the plan over all your employees. If your employees are sharing in the cost of the coverage, this is a good time to even it out.

Insurance Insights

Young males in your company, who are already relatively cheap to insure, might not realize significant savings when they move to an HDHP. The insurance companies do not expect them to use their low deductible coverage anyway, so moving to a high deductible plan doesn't change the premium very much. The females and older males with families may see a tremendous savings. By going to composite rates, you can spread around some of this savings and encourage everyone to make the change. It is also easier to administer and calculate employee contributions.

The smaller your company is, the more volatile composite rates will be. Each person who joins or leaves the group can have a big influence on the rate if they don't happen to be right in the middle of the range of rates. This is important as you are shopping for coverage. If your census changes right before the policy is issued, rates can change. After the policy is issued the rates will remain constant for the policy year.

HDHP Start Date Affects HSA Contributions

The first year that an employee chooses an HDHP, they are eligible to open an HSA during the first full month that their HDHP is effective. The amount that they may deposit in the HSA for that tax year is reduced by $\frac{1}{12}$ for each month that they did not have the HDHP coverage.

Example: An employee elects coverage with a $2,000 deductible HDHP on October 1, 2006. He also opens an HSA on the same day. His maximum contribution to his HSA of $2,000 is reduced by $1,500 ($\frac{9}{12}$ of $2,000) for the nine months that he wasn't covered by an HDHP. So he may deposit $500 anytime between October 1, 2006 and April 15, 2007.

The problem with this is that the insurance company is not permitted to reduce his deductible on his plan accordingly. If the employee is hospitalized on November 1, he will no doubt have a $2,000 deductible to pay, but will only have $500 in his HSA to use toward that deductible. The remaining

$1,500 will need to come from after-tax money or be reimbursed from future year contributions.

The truth is that many low deductible plans have at least a $1,500 out-of-pocket maximum that would rarely be tax deductible. So the employee is not really worse off with the HDHP, but the perception is hard to overcome without good communication. We discuss several strategies for overcoming this obstacle, along with other cash flow strategies, in Chapter 8.

The main concern here is that the later in the calendar year you install an HDHP, the less you can contribute to an HSA in that year. It makes January 1 the perfect day to begin an HDHP for tax reasons, even though it may be difficult for some businesses due to year-end rushes or seasonal holidays to fit in this project.

When to Make the Change

The easiest time to make the change with your current carrier is at your renewal date. Some carriers allow changes in other months during your contract year. Some require you to get permission from them. You may move to a new carrier any month that you select.

I encourage you to ignore your renewal date for a moment and think about the earliest date in the year when the preceding three months permit you the time and focus to fully explore this strategy. If October, November, and December are your busiest months, you do not want to try to make the switch on January 1. You may need to wait until March or April to be able to do it well.

Insurance Insights

Health-insurance contracts are yearly contracts, in most cases. The insurance company is bound to provide you coverage at the contractual rates, but you are not bound to accept that coverage for the entire year. You may cancel the contract, usually with 30 days advance notice, any month you choose. Contracts for larger employers and with Health Maintenance Organizations may be more restrictive. Before you plan any changes, read your contract.

After you decide on a good month to make the change, check with your current carrier to see if you can make a change at that time. It is likely, for instance, that they would not let you make the change during the last three months of your contract year. You already know that any other carrier would love to have you any month you choose.

If you do decide that you are interested in a January 1 start date, remember that the rest of the world prefers that date as well. I suggest that you start pulling together your census and looking at

plan designs as early as September 1. Set a target
date of December 1 to have all your paperwork
in to both the HDHP and HSA providers. Many
insurance companies all but shut down the last two
weeks of December. You will want your employees
to have their new insurance cards and HSA account
numbers before the world disappears.

Finding and Evaluating Insurance Companies

If you currently have a group health-insurance plan
in place at your company, you either bought it
directly from the company, through an association,
or from a broker. If you would like to look outside
that source for some comparison plans, the best
place to start is at your state insurance department.
Every state has one, and you can find their web
addresses and phone numbers in Appendix E.
I've also listed the largest insurance companies
that currently offer HDHPs in Appendix C.

You can obtain a list of all insurance companies
licensed to sell health insurance in your state. You'll
quickly recognize maybe a dozen of the names on
the list. Some only sell individual policies. Some
only sell or service very large employers. Most of
those selling group plans to small employers offer
HDHP plans. A quick call to each of the companies and you will have a short list of those that you
might do business with.

Insurance Insights

All insurance companies are rated by AM Best at www.ambest.com. A+ is the best rating given to the largest companies with the strongest financial position. A and A– are also good ratings. B+ is a good rating for a smaller company with a good financial position. Some of the smaller health insurers who do not handle other lines of coverage may find it difficult to achieve an A rating.

When reviewing insurance companies and plans, consider these criteria:

- Number of complaints filed against the company
- Helpfulness of their website
- Claim processing turnaround time
- Years in business
- Strength of their network in your city

Plan Designs

By now you understand that the complexity of this system stems from the fact that there are two contracts to manage. The difficulty moving from your current plans to HDHP/HSA plans is mostly in shedding old habits and expectations. Once you make the transition, the insurance contract is relatively simple. Once you have narrowed down the companies that you trust, there are really only five main features to look at: deductibles, co-insurance rates, preventive care, prescription co-payments, and networks. All policies have internal limits (such as the number of chiropractic visits) that may be important to you as well. But for the majority of your employees, these five will cover most of what is important to them.

Insurance Insights

Consumer-Driven Health Care is taking different forms at different insurance companies and third-party administrators. Many are adding services through web and phone access that empower employees to learn more about their care options. The aim is to keep future costs down.

Deductibles

By definition the deductibles on HDHPs are between $1,050 and $5,250 for individual coverage ($2,100 and $10,500 for family coverage). Many companies offer plans with deductibles at $1,000 intervals ($1,100, $2,000, $3,000, $4,000, and $5,000), with additional deductible levels in between $1,100 and $3,000, especially around the maximum HSA contribution limit. These deductible limits are subject to a yearly indexed increase calculated by the IRS.

Some only offered embedded deductibles that we discussed in Chapter 2. With these deductibles each individual in the family might have a separate deductible of $2,000, instead of the family needing to meet a $4,000 deductible before the insurance coverage begins.

I call plans with deductibles between $1,100 and $1,500 *Starter HDHPs*. These deductibles cause less sticker shock when employees think about how much they will need to manage themselves before the insurance coverage begins to pay claims. It's often the case that the premium savings between a current HMO or PPO and the new HSA will be almost enough to fund the maximum HSA contribution.

Example: Advanced Company has 10 employees and a monthly insurance premium of $5,000 for their HMO coverage. They switch to an HDHP with a $1,100 deductible. Their new premium of $4,100 per month saves them $10,800 per year, which they can divide up and deposit into each employees' HSA. The employees would only need to contribute $20 to make the maximum $1,100 contribution.

Deductibles between $1,500 and $3,000 are less likely to see comparable premium savings. There will be some, but it is unlikely that every employee would use $3,000 of medical care in a given year. Plans in this range would still provide significant premium savings over current plans. They also allow a higher contribution to each HSA.

Deductibles over $3,000 are the least expensive plans but may not be attractive to employees until they have had a year or two to build up a balance in their HSAs to use in the event of a major medical expense.

Co-Insurance Rates and Out-of-Pocket Maximums

As noted in Chapter 2, after the deductible is met, the insurance company can share the costs of care with the employee until the employee's share totals a specific dollar amount. The percentage that the insurance company pays is called the co-insurance rate. The specific dollar amount the employee is responsible to pay is called the out-of-pocket maximum. With HDHP plans the out-of-pocket maximum includes the deductible amount.

Example: an HDHP has a $1,100 deductible, an 80 percent co-insurance rate, and a $1,500 out-of-pocket maximum. The employee would pay the first $1,100. Then they would pay 20 percent of the next $2,000, which is $400. Their $1,000 deductible and $400 co-insurance cost total their $1,500 out-of-pocket maximum. Then the insurance company would pay 100 percent after that.

Over the years the PPO plans have offered co-insurance rates from 100 percent down to 50 percent, and out-of-pocket maximums from the deductible (on 100 percent plans) to $10,000 or more. HPHPs are limited to $5,250 out-of-pocket maximums for individuals and $10,500 out-of-pocket for families.

The initial plan offerings from the major insurance companies were limited to 100 percent and 80 percent co-insurance rates. On a 100 percent plan, the deductible and the out-of-pocket maximum is the same amount. This means that if your deductible is at or below the IRS maximum contribution to an HSA, you can fund your entire out-of-pocket maximum. Employees seem to like this type of plan. It is simple to understand and remember.

The 80 percent plans are less expensive than the 100 percent plans. This additional premium savings allows employers to contribute more to the employees' HSA accounts. This trade off is attractive to relatively young and healthy employees. They do not attach much meaning to the current out-of-pocket amounts on their PPOs and won't be concerned about the potential risk on their HDHP. They will, however, be excited about more employer money going into their HSAs.

The easiest method of comparing all plans starts with looking at all the 100 percent plans offered. See which one makes the most sense to your employees. Then, if the premium savings does not realize enough cash to fund the HSAs to the level you would prefer, consider stepping down to an 80 percent plan for a year or two, which will give you more cash to jumpstart the HSAs.

Preventive Care

We all know that an ounce of prevention is worth a pound of cure. And we love it when that prevention is covered in full with some insurance contracts. But it is still a hassle to take off work and get to the doctor. And some of the tests just aren't very pleasant. Some Washington policy makers thought that employees would not routinely get their preventive care if they a) had to fund it themselves or b) had to use cash provided by their employer in their HSA. So they made an exception to the rule prohibiting insurance payments for services before a $1,100 deductible is met. The exception is called a preventive care benefit.

An employer can add this bell (or is it a whistle?) to their group plan for an extra premium. By purchasing a preventive care benefit, in essence, they are sending money to the insurance company, which the insurance company holds on to until the employee goes to the doctor. I'm not really sold on this provision because it isn't insurance. It is prepayment for expected expenses. The other challenge is that insurance companies are very vague about defining these benefits, so it is hard to compare policies across the board and hard to educate employees. It would be far more efficient if the money was deposited in the employees' HSAs, so they could then use it to pay for preventive care as they need it.

If you have found enough money to fund the entire deductible and want to help your employees preserve their money for future year's expenses, then buying a preventive care benefit makes sense. But only if you feel your employees would value it, use it, and not be upset when it doesn't pay for everything they thought it might cover. Otherwise you are just throwing money at the insurance company.

Insurance Insights _____

The rules regarding what qualifies as preventive care include drugs used to prevent disease. This means that preventive drugs will not be subject to the deductible. Your pharmacy benefit provider may offer this option and you may find that your employees value it.

Prescription Benefits

Prior to hitting the deductible, prescription drugs costs are treated like any other expense. The employee may need to pay cash for them, using their HSA or other funding source, up to the deductible. Once the deductible is met, the insurance company will reimburse the employee at the co-insurance rate until the out-of-pocket maximum is met.

There is a significant difference evolving in how prescription benefits are received by the employees.

Some insurance contracts require the employee to purchase each prescription and then submit a claim for reimbursement, if the deductible has been met. An employee who is faced with a serious illness might have to finance several hundred dollars of prescriptions while waiting for reimbursement from the insurance company. Other contracts make information available to the pharmacist electronically and do not require payment when the employee picks up the prescription.

Word Doctor _____

The term **nonformulary** refers to a drug that's not included in the insurance company's preferred drug list. HSA funds can be used to pay the extra costs of these drugs, even though they may not count toward the deductible.

Some plans offer a drug card for use after the deductible is met. Instead of paying 20 percent (on an 80 percent plan) or the employee pays for the drug with the drug card along with a co-payment, which might be $15, $25, or $40, depending upon the type of drug. These co-payments are figured into the out-of-pocket maximum.

In almost all scenarios this means more expense for the employee when they pick up that prescription.

So it should also mean a lower premium for the policy. If you have employees who don't regularly take expensive maintenance prescriptions (e.g., high cholesterol, arthritis, etc.) then this provision will likely not make a difference to anyone. But it would save you some on the premium.

Networks

I've decided that the definition of a good network is one that has your and your spouse's doctors (and the hospitals where they practice) in it. You don't want to have to change doctors to get the network rates. And you don't want to make your employees change doctors, either.

Almost all insurance companies list their networks in searchable formats on their websites. In most cases you can search this database before you are a policyholder. If you poll your employees and ask for the names of doctors that they regularly see, you can search to see which are in the network of a company you are considering. You can also see which hospitals in your area are in network. The websites of the major insurance companies are listed in Appendix C.

If you choose to see a doctor not in the network, a separate deductible applies. There will not be a discount off their usual fee for services. This all sounds very bad, but there is a silver lining with HSAs.

Word Doctor _____

An **out-of-network provider** is a medical-services provider that has not signed a contract with a specific insurance company to provide services at agreed upon rates.

Let's say that there is a specialist that you want to see and she's so important and busy that she isn't in any networks. With an HSA you can use your tax-deductible funds to pay her. There won't be a discounted rate and her fees won't apply to your regular deductible, but you got the service you wanted, and you paid for it with pre-tax dollars.

Many employees who never go to traditional physicians because they prefer alternative therapies are very excited to have HSA funds to pay for them. They know that these expenses will not apply to the insurance deductible, but they would have incurred these expenses anyway. Before HSAs they paid the providers with after-tax dollars. Now they can use pre-tax dollars, effectively reducing the cost of these services by up to 40 percent. This is an important piece of returning control to the consumer.

The Least You Need to Know

- When you participate in an HSA, you are buying two contracts: an HDHP and an HSA. You can buy them from the same or different vendors.

- Changing to an HDHP/HSA combination takes more time than other plan changes. Give yourself at least 90 days.

- You can find health-insurance companies through your state insurance commissioner.

- HDHPs have five main provisions to consider: deductibles, out-of-pocket maximums, preventive care, prescription benefits, and networks.

Chapter 6

Smart Shopping for HSAs

In This Chapter

- How to evaluate an HSA's features
- Where to look for these accounts
- Strategies to consider when making the change

Hands on the buzzers! Name one thing you like about your checking account! Survey says:

- Had it a long time
- Free
- Know my banker
- Like the statements
- Do everything online

Did you get one right? Would you play or pass if your employees were the audience that had been polled? Do you know what is important to them about bank accounts? If you would have passed, it's time to take a real poll and stop guessing.

Features of HSAs

You are adding a new account to your employees' lives that *they* will have to manage. Even though they will own these accounts, it is likely that you will be making most, if not all, of the initial decisions, including choosing the trustee. Let's look at the features and functions your employees will care deeply about.

Fees

Years ago banks made most of their money by charging interest to their loan customers. They wanted to attract deposits because it increased the amount they could loan out by almost five times. Charging the depositor a fee seemed counterproductive to that goal. But on accounts that do not have consistently high balances, banks need to charge fees to cover their costs. HSA accounts are expected to be money in/money out accounts for the most part, at least for the first year or two. This places them in the category of account that must charge fees since they will not carry high enough balances to earn interest for the bank.

Fees will be divided into four main areas:

- Set-up
- Maintenance
- Transactions
- Services

Set-up fees are quickly disappearing from the market, but may continue on accounts that pay a commission to your broker. These fees range from $20 to $50 per account.

Maintenance fees range from $0 to $5 per month. Free regular checking accounts are relatively common across the country, so any number over $0 tends to raise eyebrows among employee groups. This seems to be the fee that is quoted most often when comparing accounts. Remember, though, that banks need to make their money somehow, so accounts with no monthly maintenance charge will either have a minimum balance requirement or make up their costs on the transaction fees.

Insurance Insights

The recent proliferation of free checking account promotions began when a clever marketing strategist figured out that people who were attracted to free checking accounts were more likely to bounce checks. The banks more than made up the lost $8 monthly maintenance fee by charging $30 every time a check bounced. HSAs have overdraft charges as well.

Transaction fees are the most complicated area to evaluate when comparing HSAs. Since employees are not used to checking accounts that have a per check transaction fee, make sure you know what's ahead for them. The fee per check can be high on HSAs. Most accounts do not charge a transaction fee for debit card uses. This is probably due to the fact that the bank receives a fee from the merchant.

Also debit card transactions are less costly to process. They may, however, charge an ATM fee for cash withdrawals.

Service fees vary from bank to bank as well. As with all kinds of accounts, check printing fees are very common but a book of starter checks may be included with the set-up fee. Additional and replacement debit cards might carry a fee. Some banks charge for a paper statement, preferring to e-mail or provide statements online. They are smart enough not to state it this way, however. They might offer an "e-account" with no monthly maintenance fee and a "basic account" that includes a paper statement and a monthly fee.

Interest Rates

The second most identifiable number on HSA accounts is their stated interest rates. Rates typically change with the Federal Reserve rates, often on a daily basis, but some of the national players that have been acquired by insurance companies or are partnering with insurance companies are taking a different approach to quoting rates. They pick a number that they think will get your attention—say, 4 percent. You know that you can't earn a guaranteed 4 percent on any liquid funds in any regular FDIC insured savings account at the moment, so you might be skeptical. You might think that this is a teaser rate that will go away the minute you sign up. It is probably a more calculated market strategy. Because these HSA providers offer the insurance side of the equation as well, they can afford to take a loss on the HSA as they make it up with the insurance premiums.

Insurance Insights

If you've ever walked into a car dealership believing that the zero percent financing they were offering was real, then you can understand what is going on here. The car dealer raises the price of the car to be able to rebate the finance company their lost interest.

Investment Choices

Employees who immediately grasp the long-term implications of the tax-free features of HSA accounts will quickly move to the question of where they can invest the funds. Insurance companies and banks that were already aggressive players in the mutual fund market quickly began offering a variety of fund options to their HSA account holders. For many of the larger insurance companies that specialize in health insurance (e.g., Blue Cross/Blue Shield affiliates), investments are a brand new game, and their banking partners have not been as quick to offer a variety of investment choices. Some initially placed minimum deposit requirements on the accounts before the funds could be diversified. As we discuss strategies in Chapter 10, you'll see that this isn't a bad idea. But it doesn't hurt to know what range of products will be available when you reach that minimum deposit amount.

Here is another aspect of the HSA management puzzle where employers may be uncomfortable. Pension rules have drilled in the notion that the employer has fiduciary responsibility for pooled funds. Even 401(k) employee contributions that the employees elect themselves point back at the employer if the employee did not have enough choices or enough education about the choices. But HSA money is the employee's money the second it hits the account, and the employer is not responsible for improper investment decisions or lack of investment options.

Does that mean that you, as an employer, don't have to put any effort into finding a reliable, responsible HSA account trustee? Of course not! Does it mean that you don't allow their representatives enough time and access to your employees to help them make good decisions? Again, no. You should, in fact, pick the fiduciary with your workforce in mind. Do they all love online banking and the ability to move investments frequently? Or do they want simplicity in their choices and a branch down the street where they can sit down with an investment specialist when they have questions?

Location

All banking used to be local. So local, in fact, that if you had to drive more than a couple of miles to your bank's branch, it seemed like a long way. Then ATMs and online banking brought our banks even closer to us. And all those branches turned into restaurants or used car dealers.

Insurance companies, on the other hand, have always been far away for most of us. And even if the home office is down the street you still didn't walk in the door to pay your premium. Instead you deal with an agent or directly with the company via the phone or Internet.

Insurance Insights

A key issue for local banks has been the adaptation of their banking and record-keeping software to accommodate HSAs. The major software vendors are ready with the versions that will allow smaller banks to offer HSAs. Watch for local banks to market HSAs aggressively once their software is installed.

How many of your employees have never seen their bank nor met their car insurance agent? This will help you know if they will be comfortable with a distance-only banking relationship. If they think of this account as a mini-health-insurance policy, they might not mind that it is far away. It's good to check with them before you select the bank.

Debit Cards

Most HSA fiduciaries offer a debit card (or two) automatically and only provide checks if the account holder asks for them. Some small local banks may start the accounts with a starter check set, as has been the custom with all checking accounts, and then send the debit card later.

Even though the account will only have one owner, banks permit a second card to be issued in another person's name. This comes in handy if your employee's spouse is usually the parent who takes the kids to the doctor or picks up the prescriptions at the pharmacy.

As noted in Chapter 5, debit cards make record-keeping a cinch. When they are used at a medical office or pharmacy, the name of that provider will appear on the bank statement. Purchases at other stores or withdrawals of cash, however, will still need back-up documentation in case of an audit.

Statements

Many HSA trustees do not mail out monthly statements; instead account holders must go online to view and print their statements. This adds an element of management that many people find cumbersome. Would your employees remember to do this? Do they have Internet service in their homes that is reliable enough to allow them consistency in accessing these records?

Insurance Insights _____

The 10 percent excise tax on nonqualified withdrawals does not apply to individuals over the age of 65 or under the age of 65 and disabled.

How to Find an HSA Provider

As you shop for HDHPs, insurance companies will tell you about their preferred HSA partners. Some may share two or more with you. Use their fees and features as benchmarks. Read their marketing material and begin to compare their features.

A few of the HSA trustees will only be available if you work with a particular insurance company. Others will sell you HSAs regardless of where you buy your insurance contract. Pay closer attention to these.

National Banks

For purposes of this discussion, a national bank is one that you can do business with via the Internet regardless of whether they have branches in your area. It might be a rather small bank, by comparison, but has found a niche with these HSA accounts.

Several national banks cut their teeth on the great-granddaddy of HSAs, the Medical Savings Accounts (MSAs). Not to be confused with Flexible

Spending Accounts, MSAs were sleepers. The laws regarding them were very restrictive and very few were opened. So it doesn't take much for a bank to claim that they have a lot of experience with MSAs. But it is something, and might give you some added confidence in their ability to service HSAs well.

 HSA Hazards

> No one sold an HSA before January 1, 2004, so if a bank claims more years of experience than that, they are counting their sales of MSAs.

I have included a list of the major players in this piece of the market in Appendix D. You can also search for trustees that service your area sorted by criteria important to you at www.hsainsider.com.

Local Institutions

For our definition of local institutions, let's reverse the criteria. A local institution is any bank that has a building in your area where an account holder can make deposits, regardless of how far the bank's market reaches and how much of their business is through the Internet.

It may seem obvious, but call your bank first. See what they are up to. They may have the accounts, but only for policyholders of a specific insurance

company. See if they want your business and what
features their accounts have. See what they are
willing to adjust to fit your needs. And ask them if
they will come to your place of business to open
the accounts in person, rather than having your
employees parade down to their branch to sign the
cards.

Next ask your employees where they bank and
check out those institutions. Then go down the
block. You may find that the new kid in town is
very aggressive with these accounts as a way to
establish their presence in town and get your other
business.

Strategies to Consider

No doubt you will pick the HDHP first, and then
evaluate HSA options. But at some point in the not
too distant future you may be re-evaluating your
HDHP selection, probably at the next renewal
date. Do you keep your HSAs where they are?
If you have a lot of employees, moving all those
accounts would be a pain in the accounting department. If you're happy with your HDHP but dis-
pleased with the HSA service, you can move the
HSAs without touching your HDHP. There are a
couple more issues to consider before you make
your final decision.

The One-Two Punch

When looking for the first HSA your employees will need, it is likely to have all the characteristics of a checking account. Accounts that look more like savings, Certificates of Deposits, Money Markets, and other Mutual Fund accounts will have different uses that won't fill the needs of most of your employees in the first year. Trying to find an account that meets all the long-term investment diversification needs in the first year may not be that important.

Even though these accounts are set up to be individual accounts with no fiduciary responsibility assigned to the employer, that doesn't prevent an employee from trying to sue you if an investment fails. One strategy to avoid this headache would be to purposefully seek out a bank that has no investment options other than fully insured certificates of deposit. You could make your employer contributions to this institution. Then let your employees know that when they accumulate an amount they don't expect to need in the short run, they can roll it over to any institution they select. There would be no trail leading back to you if the investments at the second fiduciary fail.

The Fee Dilemma

Let's say that you select an HDHP with a $1,100 deductible. Pretty standard starter plan. The HSA you select has reasonable fees, but even so they may add up to over $50 in the first year. The employee is limited to making a $1,100 deposit into the HSA based on the deductible of the HDHP. So where do the banking fees come from? The $1,100, unfortunately. This means that the employee will not have the entire deductible amount to use in the event they incur medical expenses over the deductible because the fees will have been withdrawn from that amount. Effectively, the employee may not bank their entire deductible, net of fees.

If employees use their entire deductible each year, they will come up short by the amount of the banking fees—in this case, $50. This problem will be the greatest concern to employees with low deductibles who expect their expenses to exceed their deductible each year. If any money is left over at the end of the year, it will carry forward and pre-sumably, be enough to cover the next year's fees. It is also possible that their balance will grow to the point where maintenance fees are waived.

The IRS allows account holders to pay fees directly to the institution (rather than have the institution withdraw the fees from the account), but not many banks offer this option. It wouldn't hurt to ask whether your bank offers this option, though, especially if you are selecting a lower deductible HDHP and most of your employees expect to use it up each year.

Using Your Insurance Broker

Some HSA fiduciaries pay a small finders fee to insurance brokers, which may come from the set-up fee on the account. Before you dismiss such an expense as unnecessary, remember that this is an entirely new adventure for your employees, and having a knowledgeable broker on board may save you a lot of time and a bottle of Tylenol. You may be depending upon your broker to advise you on the best HSAs for your company. Of course, you will be more likely to receive objective advice if you pay a fee to a consultant who doesn't work for commission.

 HSA Hazards

> It is getting harder and harder to tell the difference between an insurance company, an investment company, their brokers, consultants and third-party administrators. Many websites that appear to be HSA trustees are in fact insurance brokers selling these accounts.

Chex Systems

If you don't know what Chex Systems is, next time you visit your bank, look around. It won't take you too long to spot the little sign, "For your protection, we subscribe to Chex Systems." I've never understood the "your" part of that sign, but Chex

Systems does protect *the bank* from folks who have abused or defrauded banks in the past.

Chex Systems keeps a database, similar to a credit file, and searches it for a fee every time a bank opens an account. The banks usually decline to do business with folks listed in the database. If declined, an individual has a right to see his or her file and ask for any corrections of invalid information.

If you have any employees who are "unbanked" (an official term of the Federal Reserve Bank) and still conduct their business with cash or money orders, they may be doing this because they are listed in Chex Systems. Or they just may not like or understand banks.

Some banks offering HSAs do not run names through Chex Systems. Instead they protect themselves by disallowing deposits at ATMs. This is where they are exposed to the highest probability of fraud, so they have eliminated that possibility entirely.

If you suspect that any of your employees have a negative Chex System file, ask the banks you are considering whether they use this service for these accounts. Some bankers have told me that they do, but will be lenient, especially if the business is a good customer. If they are not lenient and decline to open an account for one of your employees, you would need to find another institution that will open the account for that employee. This is mostly a concern if you are using employer money to fund the accounts and need to keep the deposits comparable across your employees.

Premium Advice

Chex Systems is governed by the Fair Credit Reporting Act, which requires that they correct any errors in a reasonable amount of time. Because consumers do not regularly check their reports at this bureau and it may have been years since they last opened a bank account, there are likely to be errors that haven't been caught.

The Least You Need to Know

- Poll your employees to see what is important to them about bank accounts before you begin shopping.
- Accounts have four main types of fees to consider: set-up, maintenance, transactions, and services.
- Interest rates and investment choices may not be the most important criteria when initially setting up the accounts.
- Choosing between a national bank and a local institution may make the most difference in the long run.

Chapter 7

Controlling Company Costs

In This Chapter

- Evaluating the true cost of compensation
- Finding the best plan starting with fixed costs
- Long-term cost analysis of HSA strategies

The cost of group health insurance is rising at a rate much faster than the general inflation rate. Employers have not seen the market for their services increase comparatively, leaving them few comfortable options to fund these cost increases. Bringing employees back into the decision-making process by making them aware of the true cost of health care may be the most logical first step to getting control of health insurance costs.

Contributory vs. Voluntary Benefit Plans

When employee benefits began to gain popularity in the 1960s and 1970s, business used them to spice up compensation offers to help attract good workers. Employers were able to buy insurance products at below market rates because the insurance companies incurred fewer marketing costs to sell their policies to one employer with 20 people instead of 20 individual policies.

Cost may not be the driving force anymore. For many people, especially those who are young and healthy, rates could actually be cheaper for individual plans than for group plans. For many, the issue is now access and plan features. Individual health policies are carefully underwritten, meaning that many people with seemingly benign conditions (e.g., mild depression) might be turned down for coverage. Groups can provide access to health insurance that some cannot get on their own. Group plans also carry a variety of options not available on individual plans. One major carrier sells only 2 different plans to individuals, but offers 17 different plans to small groups and a virtually unlimited number of options to large groups. When an employer offers health insurance through a group plan, they have to offer it to every full-time employee (as defined by their state). The employer has to offer comparable coverage (and also *comparable contributions* to HSAs) to *comparable participating employees*. The insurance company has to accept each employee for coverage, regardless of the employee's health status, if they have issued a policy to the group. Individual policies do not usually have that insurability guarantee, resulting in lower premiums in many cases.

Word Doctor

Comparable participating employees are those covered by your HDHP and eligible to establish an HSA, who fall in the same category of coverage (single, family) and the same category of employment (part-time, full-time).

The IRS defines **comparable contributions** as either the same amount or the same percentage of the deductible for each participating employee. Contributions that are not comparable are subject to a 35 percent excise tax.

Group coverage requires a minimum participation level—typically 50 percent of the full-time employees. Many employers are now finding that some employees will opt to keep their individual policy rather than pay toward a group plan. Interestingly, these employees often do not expect to be compensated in another way for the compensation they are losing by not joining the group insurance plan. Some employers offer some sort of modest payment to those employees, but usually find they are less expensive to employ.

Over the years most employers have stopped offering free health insurance to their employees. Instead they usually offer one of three standard billing arrangements:

- A *contributory* plan is one that the employer contributes all or some of the premium (usually at least 50 percent).

- A *voluntary* plan is one in which the entire premium withheld from an employee's paycheck. These plans are usually offered for ancillary benefits, such as dental or disability insurance. They may have some of the features of group insurance, such as minimum participation and relaxed underwriting.

- A *list bill* is a system in which the employee is the owner of an individual policy and has the entire premium withheld from their paycheck. Employers may not contribute to these premiums.

Premium Advice _____

If you choose to offer insurance through a list billing, the employee must pay the entire insurance premium, but you can contribute to the HSA on their behalf, as long as you do not discriminate across employees.

Calculating Total Compensation

Let's pretend that I am your employee. I do a great job as your top sales person and bring in $300,000 gross revenue for your business. You have debt payments, overhead, marketing, inventory, and other costs that have to come out of that $300,000. You also have to pay yourself, my manager and my support staff. Your competitor down the street is willing to pay me $75,000 to work for them, so you try to keep my salary near that target.

But what do I really cost you? There are a lot of ways to look at this, but let's evaluate my salary, employer taxes, and benefits by calculating actual cash going out the door:

Salary	$75,000
Employer FICA	$5,738
Unemployment	$1,875
Workers' Compensation	$1,500
Retirement Fund	$2,250
Health Insurance	$4,200
Life/Disability Insurance	$600

It costs you over $90,000 to pay me a $75,000 salary. When you hired me you knew I would cost this much and you expected that I would produce at least three times that amount in sales. So you offered me the job as $75,000 plus benefits. If I hit your sales target, you would have enough to pay me a nice bonus at the end of the year, and keep me from going to work for your competitor.

When Costs Rise

Fast forward to the following year. Sales are down a bit and even though I'm still at the top of the leader board, I'm only bringing in $270,000. Your renewal notice from the health-insurance carrier arrives announcing a 30 percent increase in the premium. I'm going to cost you another $1,260 per year, but my production indicates you can only afford to spend a total of $90,000 for me.

Here are your choices:

- Lay me off and find someone who can produce more revenue.
- Reduce my salary.
- Eliminate or reduce contributions to the retirement fund.
- Eliminate or reduce contributions to the health plan.
- Eliminate or reduce contributions to the life or disability insurance.

Assuming you want to keep me, you should be indifferent between the other four options. Your goal is to keep your cost for my services within a range that will permit you to realize a profit. You are also constrained by the nondiscrimination rules that require you to offer similar benefit options to all your employees.

I most definitely have different goals that cause me to see the other four options very differently. Since you have been paying the premiums for the health, life, and disability insurance, I am not accustomed to thinking about those benefits as a number that can be added to my salary to determine my cost to you. If I am now asked to pay a portion of these benefits, it will feel like a pay cut to me.

We have a problem. I am not generating enough revenue to justify my cost. But part of my cost has been hidden from me until now, so I am not happy about considering cuts in my benefits as a solution to keep costs in check. What started out as a nice benefit package has now turned into a battle. I feel I deserve to have health insurance. You know it is still your job to keep the company profitable or there won't be a job left to offer me, with or without benefits.

Whose Money Is It?

This entire argument can be reduced to the simple question, "Whose money is it?" Employees want their employers to pay for stuff. Employers are often heard exclaiming that they can't afford this stuff anymore. It seems that we have drawn some artificial lines between what is the employer's money and the employee's money. Even the insurance companies have added to the confusion by requiring a certain portion of premiums be paid by the employer for certain types of policies (contributory).

Think about it this way. Every dime you spend to compensate and motivate an employee is no longer your money. It is part of the total compensation cost you bear that buys you that employee's productivity. If their cost goes up, but their productivity does not, you can't afford them. It makes absolutely no difference whether that money is paid to them in their gross pay or paid as a separate check written to their disability insurance provider. It is still no longer your money.

There are some differences in tax calculations for several benefits depending upon whether you pay the employee and let them pay for the expense or you pay the bill directly on their behalf. Knowing these differences can help you save money on the cost of your employee, but that is all. It is still no longer your money.

The gap here is that employees do not think about the money you spend on their behalf as their money. They like to think about it as your money. They like to think that it is reducing your gross income, not theirs. But as a good business manager, you know your costs and your acceptable profit margin. You would be thrilled to just give me a check for $90,000 (in the preceding example) and let me pay all my taxes and my insurance premiums. This, in fact, is why employers still try to get away with treating employees as contractors even after the IRS tightened up those regulations years ago.

As we discuss the complications that HSA deposits bring to this conversation, I'd like you to work with the following two assumptions:

- All the money spent on insurance benefits is part of your total cost of compensation and as such, is the employee's money.

- The employees are happiest when they believe that it is your money being spent.

Premium Advice

If you have not done a comprehensive evaluation of your compensation costs recently, now would be a good time to do that. If you are feeling stressed by the costs of health insurance, finding out how that contributes to your overall compensation costs will be helpful. The same holds true for each employee. If they are stressed out about their health-care and health-insurance costs, they can gain some insight by looking at their overall budget.

HSA Funding Strategies

It is important to think through the basics of how you design your compensation strategies before you implement an HDHP/HSA strategy. In the past you had the following formula to work out:

Insurance Cost = Employer Contribution + Employee Contribution

Even though we have agreed that it is all employee money paying for this cost, you still had to split it up in an accounting sense, for the insurance company and the IRS.

Now with HSAs you have two formulas to reconcile:

> Insurance Cost = Employer Contribution + Employee Contribution

> Savings Deposit = Employer Contribution + Employee Contribution

Both of these pieces will be part of the overall compensation costs.

Who Pays What

It is amazing how many different ways you can divide up these costs. What is more amazing is how employees are likely to react to the different arrangements you come up with. Let's start with an example:

Joe's Company has a total compensation cost of $60,000 per month. Specifically $10,000 of that is paid to the health-insurance policy, $5,000 of the $10,000 is withheld from employee paychecks and the other $5,000 is paid out of funds separate from payroll. As far as Joe is concerned, it costs him $60,000 per month for his employees and that is what they are worth, based on their productivity. The rest is just details.

Joe's insurance company tells him he can have better benefits for his employees if he sends $6,000 per month to an HDHP and deposits $4,000 per month to savings accounts on behalf of his employees. Let's say that Joe likes the idea of consumer-driven health care and feels that since his workers are mostly healthy, they would end up with balances in their HSAs at the end of the year.

He has three general choices on how to split the payments:

- He can leave the 50/50 split the same, withholding $3,000 of the $6,000 premium and paying the rest. Also paying half of the $4,000 HSA contribution.

- He can reduce the employee withholding for the insurance to $1,000, pay the remaining $5,000, and contribute nothing to the HSAs.

- He can leave the employee withholding for the insurance at $5,000, pay the remaining $1,000 and contribute the full $4,000 to the HSAs. (Some insurance companies would object to this split because they require a minimum of 50 percent of the premium to be paid by the employer.)

From a cost perspective, he is indifferent about the three options. Each of the options keep his insurance premium costs at $10,000 and his total compensation costs at $60,000. The employees, however, will have more control over their net paycheck in the first two options. Because their contribution to the insurance portion was reduced, and the HSA contribution is voluntary, they may enjoy a bigger paycheck. In the third option the employees will see the same paycheck, but will have a guaranteed deposit to their HSA.

Joe will need to explore these different approaches with his employees. Some employees will see the flexibility of a larger paycheck and voluntary deposits to the HSA as an added benefit. Some will take the opposite opinion, arguing that they are already used to their paycheck at its current level so the forced savings into the HSA would truly benefit them. Since Joe must treat his employees similarly, he won't be able to let them pick and choose their cost sharing, but he will want to offer the option preferred by most of his employees.

Starting at the End

When you sit down to figure all this out, the best place to start is at the end. Just like any major decision you make, you need to start with the outcome you desire. For many employers, this conversation about HSAs will be prompted by an unacceptable—and unaffordable—increase in their health-insurance rates at renewal time. They will go shopping. In fact, a good agent will have them shopping a month or two before they know their renewal premium, with the assumption that rates are still skyrocketing.

Most often an employer will state his or her
goal as:

> I want to get the best insurance coverage
> I can for the least amount of money.

As my 13-year-old would say, "Duh, Mom!" Forget
that goal. It won't get you anywhere, except frustrated. The first thing it does is force you to keep
secrets. You want to shop for coverage, but you
don't want to tell anyone what you currently have
and what you spend, thinking that the quotes you
receive will only just beat your current coverage
and not really find you the best deal. The other
thing wrong with such a vague goal is that there
are two independent variables in the equation.
Both the coverage and the cost are moving
targets ... you'll never be satisfied that you have
found the optimum solution.

Deciding on Cost

So let's pick one variable—coverage or cost—to
be independent. Since coverage is impossible to
clearly define (again, too many variables) and cost
is a single number, I like to use cost. You can only
have one of three goals: keep compensation costs
constant, reduce them, or increase them. You will
know which of these three you should pick based
on the productivity of your company. Here are
some things to think about when deciding which
goal is right for you:

- If productivity is increasing, you will be most interested in retaining your productive workforce, and you will likely want to increase compensation.

- If productivity is constant, you will want to keep compensation constant.

- If productivity has decreased, you will need to reduce compensation to stay in business.

Which one is it? Higher, lower, same? Then, of that compensation cost, what portion will be dedicated to health benefits?

Finding the Best Plan for that Cost

Now ask yourself this question:

> "If my employees spend × dollars a month on health benefits, what is the best use of that money?"

This is a question you can answer! Imagine walking into a car dealer with bag full of $100 bills. You show them to the sales associate and explain that you only have $30,000 to spend on a car and you want to see the nicest car you can leave with today. If she's good, she'll start narrowing down your definition of "nicest." In order to get to the final car, you will have to make a lot of trade-offs. You can have leather seats or a DVD player, but not both.

The same thing will happen as you narrow down your insurance choices. Keeping the cost constant, you will be able to see clearly what you value and what will work for your employees. You can play with deductibles, out-of-pocket maximums, and HSA deposits. You can compare plan designs across carriers that may not have the same exact benefits.

Adjusting Cost Assumptions

If you cannot find a strategy that works (as if you had walked into the car dealer with only $500), you may need to raise your cost assumption. But keeping with our premise that your overall compensation costs are predetermined, this would mean shifting the money from other compensation expenses, such as gross pay or other benefit costs.

Do you want to keep the net cost for both employer and employee side of the compensation equation proportionate to the previous split? Or do you want to fix one at its previous level, and only move the other? For years many employers have had a level contribution from employee withholding (e.g., $50/month). They absorbed each year's renewal increase in their side of the formula. Now some employers are passing through the entire increase each year, keeping their contribution constant.

Reasons to Change

Not all employer groups will find that the HDHP/HSA combination makes sense for them. And maybe they never will. It is just as important to know when this won't work as to know when it will. For some employers, the challenge will be to take a short-term loss in order to realize a long-term gain.

Comparing Unreimbursed Expenses

As you consider the switch to HDHPs you need to make sure that your PPO option (or some new one) isn't the best place to be. Start by taking the fixed cost you have assumed in the preceding strategy. Find the PPO with the highest benefit levels that you can buy for that cost. Let's say that it has a $20 office visit co-pay, $10/20/30 prescription co-pay, $500 deductible, 80/20 percent to $1,500 out-of-pocket plan. And let's say that the same money will buy an HDHP/HSA that includes a $1,500 deductible, 100 percent HDHP plan with a $1,000 HSA contribution.

In a rainy year, with the PPO plan an employee will have approximately $2,000 of after tax expenses (out-of-pocket plus estimated co-pays). In the HDHP, he will have a $500 potential pretax expense to cover all his expenses ($1,500 deductible less $1,000 HSA contribution). He comes out $1,500 ahead with the HDHP.

In a sunny year, the PPO plan will cost approximately 100 dollars in routine office visits and prescriptions. The HDHP would leave him with approximately $400 in his HSA after paying for the same office visits and prescriptions. This year he comes out $500 ahead with the HDHP.

There are some fair to partly cloudy years where the deductible might be met under an HDHP, but the PPO costs would still be just a few co-payments. Be aware that these scenarios will be the ones that employees spend the most amount of time analyzing. It is hard to predict every possibility and prove that an HDHP will leave them better off. The probability is that the sunny years will leave enough cushion in the HSA to get through the years in between.

Controlling Renewal Rates

We all understand the notion of compound interest: interest computed on last year's interest. It's a good thing, if you are on the earning side. Compounding is a very bad thing when it comes to insurance rates, however. Let's look at an example:

The Green Company has a PPO plan that costs $7,000 per month. Their 18 percent renewal raises that premium to $8,260. Over five years, renewals at this rate almost double the premium:

Today	$7,000
Next year	$8,260
Year three	$9,745
Year four	$11,501
Year five	$13,571

The Brown Company has an HDHP plan that costs $4,500 per month and they bank the other $2,500 in HSAs. Their HDHP is projected to have

7 percent renewal rates, due to the impact of the higher deductible and consumer driven decision-making. Look what happens over five years to their premiums:

Today	$4,500 HDHP + $2,500 HSA = $7,000
Next year	$4,815 HDHP + $2,500 HSA = $7,315
Year three	$5,152 HDHP + $2,500 HSA = $7,652
Year four	$5,512 HDHP + $2,500 HSA = $8,012
Year five	$5,897 HDHP + $2,500 HSA = $8,397

This is a cumulative 20 percent increase compared to the 94 percent increase the Green Company experienced with the PPO. The other factor that is hard to measure is the portion of the $150,000 banked in the HSAs over that time period that will still be there, reducing the effective cost even more. We could also add in all the co-payments the employees didn't have to make, to see an even greater return.

Increasing Deductibles as HSAs Grow

Five years down the road is not a long time for most employers to begin planning for. At that time, a percentage of the employees will have growing balances in their HSAs. Let's say that the plan you select this year has a $1,500 deductible and you deposit $1,000 per year in each employee's account. It is possible that somebody will have $5,000, plus interest earnings, in that account in five years. Not likely, but possible. Some will have none and others will have modest balances. Many will be over the $1,500 mark. This means that they can now select a higher deductible HDHP and lower the insurance cost even more.

This is truly the long-term view of these plans. Each company would have a dual option where new employees or those who do use their deductible each year could choose a plan with a lower deductible and those who have built a balance in their HSA could choose a higher deductible. When we factor in the premium savings to this type of strategy we can see costs going down in the long run. It is a very simple concept, actually. Use the insurance company's and IRS's money to fund these accounts until they provide a significant amount of self-insurance, allowing the employee to buy less insurance.

The Least You Need to Know

- The two primary benefits of group health insurance are: the coverage of individuals who might otherwise be uninsurable and the wide variety of plan designs available.

- Money spent for employee benefits is all part of the employee's compensation, whether it is paid for through payroll deduction or outside of payroll.

- An employer needs to look at plans by first calculating the amount they want to compensate that employee and shopping for plans within that cost.

- HDHP/HSA strategy is a long-term cost containment strategy that some employers may find costs them more in the first year or two.

Chapter

Cash Flow Concerns

In This Chapter

- The cash flow pitfalls of HSA funding
- Financing strategies to overcome the challenges
- Pros and cons of automatic claim forwarding

As employers listen to brokers across the country sing the praises of HSAs, they wait for the punch line. There has to be something wrong. It seems too good to be true. So here's what's wrong with this picture.

Deposits to HSAs

On the surface, the deposit rules for HSAs are very simple. Once you calculate your maximum allowable deposit, which we discussed in Chapter 3, you can put any or all of the money in the account anytime between January 1 of the tax year and April 15 of the following year.

The Funding Dilemma

It's Memorial Day and the kids are all excited to get to the pool for the first time. You find what's left of last year's pool toys and you head out. The kids run through the gate and straight to the high dive yelling, "Watch me!" You look and to your horror, there is one foot of water in the deep end.

After you safely get the children down from the diving board, you storm into the pool office and demand an explanation. The pool manager apologizes and tells you that they get to buy the same amount of water they did last year, but they can only buy $1/12$ of it each week for 12 weeks.

"What good does that do me?" you yell. "You're telling me the kids can't dive until 12 weeks from now?"

If you don't fill your employees' HSAs to the top the first month of the year, they'll feel like they are diving into a pool with a foot of water. The dilemma is that even though the funding of the HSA is very flexible, the payment of the deductible is not. If they have a plan with an $1,100 deductible and they end up at the emergency room on January 2, using $1,200 worth of services, they would need to pay the hospital $1,100. If their HSA were being funded monthly, they would only have $91.67 to apply to a $1,100 bill.

HSA Hazards

> If any of your employees have family coverage and a spouse who also has family coverage at his or her employer, their maximum contributions will be half of the lower deductible.

Mid-Year Starting Dates

Your employees might experience a similar shortfall if you install an HDHP/HSA strategy partway through the year. Back to the deposit rules, you recall that if you begin an HDHP in any month other than January you must prorate the maximum deposit allowable.

Example: You begin a $2,000 deductible HDHP in May. Since you have seven months left in the year, you may contribute $7/12$ of $2,000 to each HSA account, or $1,167. If you choose to deposit the monthly amount of $167 to each account, an employee who has a large claim immediately will find himself $1,833 short.

The Difference with PPOs

Employees coming off of PPO plans into HSA plans will immediately find their math skills improving. They can tell you exactly how much they are at risk for at any given moment. The difference between their deductible (or out-of-pocket on non-100 percent plans) and the balance in their

HSA. It is one of the wonderful side effects of this new system. They know what their risk is.

Prior to this transition, they might have had a $250 deductible and $1,000 out-of-pocket maximum with $15 office visit co-pays and $20 prescription co-pays. They would rarely do the math to calculate their risk at any given point. They didn't want to think about having to come up with $1,000 if they were in the hospital. For most, that was what credit cards were for. The most important thing to them was that it would only cost $35 if they need to see the doctor and buy some antibiotics. They could come up with $35 easily so it didn't seem like a risk.

Now everything has changed. That doctor visit and prescription could run $250. And they only have $167 in their account. This scares most people used to $15 here and $20 there. They still have the same credit card they would have charged the hospital visit to on their earlier plan, but it doesn't feel the same, for some reason.

Cash Flow Planning

It takes some education and some planning to bring people to the point where they value the fact that they now have a much lower risk over each year. Their only potential problem is one of negative cash flow in the early months. If they have no claims early in the year, it won't be a problem. If they end the year with a balance in their HSA, the potential problem next year is lessened by the amount they are carrying over.

Should this potential problem materialize into a real problem it must be financed. There are four sources of financing: the employer, the employee, the vendor, and other insurance contracts. Prior to installing your plan you should decide which source you will be using.

Employer Financing Up Front

The cleanest solution from the employee's perspective is for the employer to assume all the risk. Just put the entire deductible in the HSA at the beginning of the year. Done!

Assuming you have the cash to do this, do you want to? How stable is your workforce? Would your turnover predict that most of the money would walk out the door? Or would it be such a motivation to employees that their loyalty would be improved? I've met employers who view it both ways.

Let's say you have the cash. Everyone who works for you has been there 30 years. On top of that, there is terrible unemployment and no one hiring in your town. They are staying. Gosh, is this simple: write one check to the fiduciary on January 1 and you're done.

If someone does leave, you aren't going to get your money back. They will have to make a taxable withdrawal from the account for the months that they are no longer covered by an HDHP.

Premium Advice

Although COBRA requires you to continue to offer coverage for terminated employees if you have more than 20 of them, you are not required to pay the insurance premium. This law doesn't apply to HSAs directly. You would still need to offer the continuation of the HDHP. If they did continue coverage with your HDHP (or another) they could continue to make deposits to the HSA. You would not be required to pay anything into the HSA.

Employer Financing After the Fact

The HSA rules prohibit you from making preferential deposits. So if Mary has foot surgery in February, you can't deposit $2,000 to her HSA all at once to help her out.

But Mary is your employee and on your payroll. You can give pay advances to any employee at any time that you see fit. You could establish a hardship payroll advance policy that could help her out. This money would be taxed as other ordinary income. The taxes are reversed, in a sense, as the loan is repaid.

Mary then pays her doctor and hospital bills with money advanced to her. As Mary repays her advance, she can withdraw money from her HSA to reimburse herself for the expenses she incurred. There is no time limit on withdrawals, as long as the account was open when the expense was incurred.

Many employers like this approach, knowing that the chances are slim that very many employees will plow through their deductibles early in the year. The other very desirable feature of this strategy is that pay advances can be withheld out of final pay-checks. If they are offered as loans with loan agreements, there may be other recourse to collect them as well.

Employee Financing

How does the commercial go? "For everything else, there's MasterCard." Well, a deductible might just be one of those things that qualifies as every-thing else. You will have a sense whether your employees have access to credit lines (or credit worthy family members) equal to or greater than the deductible you picked for the HDHP.

If your employees finance their deductibles through credit card advances, they could reimburse themselves each month for the payment on the card from their HSA. Again, there is no time limit on withdrawals, so they have a lot of flexibility. Some may complain about the interest accruing but that is a predictable cost of this financing strategy.

Insurance Insights _____

Be prepared for the banks to figure out that people might need cash to cover their deductible and bundle credit and debit features together with HSAs. An employee could incur a debt when the account is low and pay it back when the contributions are made.

If the employee pays a portion of the maximum deposit to the HSA, either through payroll or outside of payroll, he or she could accelerate those deposits. The employee can move money from another saving or investment into the HSA to meet the expense incurred. The remainder of the deposits throughout the year would need to be reduced so they don't exceed the maximum allowed during that tax year.

Some employees choose to make their portion of the deposit in advance at the beginning of the year, just to pump up the balance in anticipation of ongoing expenses. This is a legitimate strategy. If you can establish the flexibility through your payroll system to do this, your employees will appreciate it. For instance, an employee who wants to deposit $1,000 per year might ask to have $250 per pay withheld for the first four paychecks and then nothing withheld the rest of the year.

Vendor Financing

Ask any doctor about their receivables and they'll tell you that they finance patient billing all the time. It will get worse, not better, with HDHP/ HSA coverage. Sometimes patients just don't pay their bills, or they take a long time to do it.

With HDHP coverage, the insurance card will not specify a co-payment required. If the vendor is in the network of the insurance company, their contract specifies that they may not ask for money in advance. The claim must be submitted and "repriced" or discounted for the network discount. This can take days or weeks to happen. When the new amount is known, they can bill the patient, who can then use their HSA to pay their portion.

What if the HSA doesn't have the money needed to pay the bill? And the patient doesn't have savings or a credit card? The vendor will have to wait for their money. The patient could offer to make payments using the HSA deposits as they are made each month. Many doctors and hospitals are used to receiving monthly payments. They don't like it any more than you like your customers to string you out, but it is an option.

Gap Insurance

We have learned that you may not have an insurance policy that pays any benefits prior to your deductible if you want to qualify to make deposits to an HSA. Just like most rules, there are exceptions. You can own what is commonly called a hospitalization policy that pays you a daily amount if you are in the hospital. You can also own specific disease policies (what we used to call cancer policies, but now are offered for other diseases as well).

The insurance industry noticed this "gap" between the amount of your deductible and the amount you are allowed to deposit into an HSA in the early months of a plan. They saw a marketing opportunity and crafted policies that would help with the problem without destroying the tax advantages of HSAs.

Automatic Claim Forwarding

In Chapter 6, we explored the pros and cons of bundling your HDHP and HSA contracts with the same company. One of the options you have with bundled products is automatic claim forwarding. It can be a wonderful enhancement to an HDHP/HSA plan, but it can also be a major pain.

The concept of bundling is similar to how Medicare works. If you purchase a Medicare supplement, the claim will be sent automatically from Medicare to the supplement insurer. Medicare pays what they will and sends that information along to the supplement. Then the supplement pays and you get an explanation of benefits (EOB).

In the case of an HDHP/HSA combination, the HDHP would get the claim first. After they determine that you haven't met your deductible yet, they check your HSA balance. If there is enough money there to pay the remainder of the claim, they draft that amount and send it along to the vendor. When you get your EOB, it states how much the insurance contract paid and how much your HSA paid. You are done. It is very simple—if there is enough money in your account.

For many people in the early months or years of their HSA, the balance will not be consistent. It will be a money in/money out account. In this case, giving the insurance company the power to automatically draft funds to pay claims could be confusing.

Example: Your bookkeeper goes to the doctor for a sprained ankle and the doctor charges her $60 for the office visit (the network negotiated rate) and sends the charges into your insurance company. He sends her to the lab for an x-ray to make sure there is no break. They charge her $150 and bill the insurance company. The doctor writes the bookkeeper a prescription for a brace for her to wear. She writes a check from her HSA for $45 and submits the claim herself to get credit toward her deductible.

In the example if the employee has automatic claims forwarding, the $60 and $150 charges will be drafted from her HSA after the insurance company applies the charges toward her deductible. If she doesn't have automatic claims forwarding, she will be billed from both providers. She will then need to send checks or call them with her debit card account number.

Word Doctor

The ultimate goal of some insurance companies is to offer you a **one swipe card**. This card would be both your debit card and your insurance card. With one swipe you could zap your HSA and file your claim.

Another challenge is the fact that checks don't always clear the account quickly. If you write a check to a doctor who holds it for a week, your insurance company may draw out that money before the check arrives, causing it to bounce. My advice is to recommend to your employees that if they choose the automatic claims forwarding option they should only use a debit card that posts immediately. Using checks will likely cause the most potential problems.

Employees may not want to elect this option for a variety of reasons. The most difficult scenario is when they are also using the account for other qualified withdrawals, such as non-network deductible expenses, insurance premiums, or dental expenses. If they have written checks for these expenses that haven't cleared, the insurance company could withdraw funds at exactly the wrong time, causing a check to bounce.

Even though it can lead to confusion, the automatic claims forwarding feature is convenient.

If you install a higher deductible plan and maximize the contribution to the accompanying HSA early in the year, never having to write a check or pay a doctor bill is rather nice. If you have funds left from last year, you might also be in a good position to take full advantage of this feature.

The Least You Need to Know

- The timing of the deposits to the HSAs may cause a shortfall in funding the deductible of the HDHP.

- Employees are much more aware of this shortfall than they were of the out-of-pocket risk they assumed on PPO plans.

- There are four financing sources for the shortfall: employer, employee, vendor, and other insurance.

- Automatic claim forwarding can be a convenience for those who have funded their accounts sufficiently and would like automatic payments out of their HSAs.

HDHP/HSA Installation

In This Chapter

- The 10 steps to converting to an HDHP/HSA plan
- Tips for making the process positive and smooth
- Troubleshooting common hot spots in the transition

If you are a list maker, this chapter will make your day. We have covered a lot of the pieces in previous chapters but it may seem that they are all jumbled together like the clean and dirty clothes on your teenager's bedroom floor. I'm going to help you sort it out and decide where you are in the process and what to do next.

Putting It All Together

I have identified 10 major steps in the process to convert to an HDHP/HSA plan. Here they are:

1. Background/strategic research
2. Introductory awareness education
3. Identifying employees who might participate
4. Locating insurance companies
5. Collecting plan designs and premiums
6. Selecting a company and a plan (or plans)
7. Determining cost sharing and cash flow
8. Specific plan education
9. Enrolling employees in HDHPs and open-
   ing HSAs
10. Follow-up support/education

Let's go through them one at a time. You will want
to schedule a minimum of three months to move
through these steps. If you have six, all the better.
I also think you will need to budget at least 20
hours of your own time to this project over that
3 to 6 months. Much of the work you can delegate
to your insurance broker, your accountant, and
your support staff, but you will be the one pulling
together the information for the final decision. So
start with a timetable that feels comfortable to you.

This change, like all major changes, will need to be
endorsed from the top down. Every employee will
want to know that you are squarely behind it and
understand the pros and cons before they jump on
board. You need to determine the tone of the message at the education sessions, which will in turn

determine the level of employee participation and commitment to the concept.

Step 1: Background/Strategic Research

Congratulations! Reading the first eight chapters of this book (assuming you didn't cheat and start at this chapter) has you well on your way to understanding the major concepts and many of the strategic issues. I have listed some additional resources in Appendix F to take you further in your analysis.

At this point in the process, you should take into account your own personal/family situation. It is best for you to sort that out first. Does your spouse fully understand what you are considering, and are there any prejudices there? This change has to make sense for you and your family first, and you may eventually find that it only makes sense for you. Many business owners move to an HSA and leave their employees at a PPO or install a Health Reimbursement Arrangement or HRA (more on that in Chapter 11).

You are involved in this research because something piqued your interest. Maybe it was simply an astronomical rise in your health-insurance premiums at your last renewal. Maybe it was the lure of the tax-free savings that you can get as a business owner. Whatever got you going, at some point you will feel comfortable enough with the concept to begin a formal analysis.

Step 2: Introductory Awareness Education

During your preliminary research it is likely you ran into a brochure or a website that summed up the concepts in a way that you felt your employees would understand. You know your employees better than anyone. Do they need excruciating detail before they believe anything (engineers, huh)? Or are they too busy to read past the first sentence of a brochure because they have places to be and people to call (your sales force, no doubt)?

Can you get all these folks together in one place at one time, or will you have to do this in a broadcast e-mail? Communication is key at this phase. The method is not as important as the message, which is:

> There is a new concept that many companies are looking at. I've found it intriguing at first glance. I'd like you to [read the attached, attend an informational session, etc.] so we can all learn about this together and decided if it might benefit our company.

Next make a list of the troublemakers in your company. I don't have to tell you who they are. Anytime anything changes, they are in your office registering their disapproval. Don't be afraid of them. Instead engage them. Assign them a role in this exploration. Make them in charge of something. Form a committee and let them complain to each other. Anything to allow them to channel their energy. It's not a bad idea to invite the spouses who are likely to complain (yours, maybe?) to join in this process as well.

You will learn a lot from this exploration process. It will look like you are educating your employees, but the goal here is for you to keep gathering information. You should be able to find out a great deal about their fears and frustrations. You will find out how they view their current plan and what they value about it. You will begin to form opinions on decisions you will make later, such as where the HSA funding should come from, how the premiums should be shared and what type of investment choices they might like.

Step 3: Identifying Employees Who Might Participate

Before you shop you will need to compile an accurate census for quoting purposes. It is impossible to create a perfect list, so don't beat yourself up. Start with the list of every full-time employee eligible for insurance. And don't limit your list to employees who are currently covered—some people who did not previously choose coverage might do so now. The lower cost, the employer contribution to the HSA, or the tax benefits might bring them onto your new plan.

Include the following information in your census:

- Employee name
- Gender
- Date of birth

- Spouse's Date of birth (if applicable)
- Number of children (if applicable)
- Who is currently covered on the plan

If there are any predictable changes, like an employee in her probationary period, a dependent who will age out, or an employee set to be married soon, you can make those adjustments to your census now. There is no doubt that your census will be different when it comes time to actually install your policy, but at least you have a good sense of where things stand now.

If your company is large enough to allow more than one plan option to your employees (usually more than 10 employees on the plan), you might want to take a straw poll at this point. After the initial education, you could ask employees to indicate their likely interest in the new design. This is a difficult question to ask because it prompts a tremendous number of follow-up questions (especially from the engineers and the spouses). You might state it conditionally:

> If we could locate an HDHP/HSA combination strategy that saved both you and the company money, but kept your out-of-pocket risk at or below our current plan, would you be interested in changing plans?

This will flush out the truly anxious among your ranks. Anyone who answers, "No," to this question is change-adverse and will probably need huge incentives to be happy about changing plans.

Your goal is to get as close as possible to two lists: "probably would take the HDHP/HSA" and "probably wouldn't take the HDHP/HSA." People will move back and forth up to the final moment and beyond, but you will have a place to start. While you are polling your employees, you could also ask them to give you the names and addresses of any physicians that they would not want to lose. You can use this data later to determine the scope of the networks you are considering.

Premium Advice

There will likely be some anxiety about switching plans in the middle of a tax year (if your policy renewal date is not January 1). Even though deductibles will likely carry forward to the new policy, the old PPO deductible did not include the office visits and prescriptions as the new one will.

If you have the opportunity to offer a dual option, you are in a wonderful position. You can keep your current plan in place and add the option of an HDHP/HSA. You may find a small number moving to the new plan the first year, and more following suit the next year as rate increases put more distance between the plans. Remember that you are installing a long-term strategy, and everything doesn't have to happen all at once.

Step 4: Locating Insurance Companies

Appendix E has information on your State Insurance Commissioner's website and consumer hotline. They will be able to provide you with a list of companies that are licensed to sell health insurance in your state. If you have employees in other states, you can obtain that state's list of licensed companies as well. Crosscheck the lists to get the list of possible providers.

You will find the major national companies offering HDHPs listed in Appendix C. You have probably heard of most of them because you have seen quotes from them in previous years. But HDHPs and HSAs have shaken up the market a bit. You may find some new ones or you may find that they have changed names, merged, or been acquired.

Next you need to evaluate networks. This is a wonderful job to give the troublemaker committee. Let them take the list of primary physicians collected in Step 3 and see which networks contain most of them. They can do this on the insurance companies' websites. The only hard part to this is that at some point they will likely be asked to choose a product type. The choices will not be self-explanatory. They may need your guidance on this. A call to the company's customer service line or local sales office explaining what you are trying to do should give you the right box to click.

Check your family's doctors first. You are a very rare bird if you move your company to an insurance plan that your doctors don't participate in. Likewise there may be key employees or those with rare medical problems who value their provider relationships. Tell your committee to keep a close watch on those providers.

Also check the major hospitals and pharmacy chains that your employees would use. Make sure you know which ones have pulled out of various networks recently. They may just be in the middle of contract negotiations and will be back shortly.

Premium Advice

While your committee is at the websites checking out the networks, also have them rate the usability of the site. Most of the sites have several features that nonpolicy holders can access. They also might have a walk-through to show them what would be available to them as policyholders. Web access is very important to the success of Consumer Directed Healthcare. Get your employees' opinions in advance.

Now you have a list of the companies offering health insurance with sufficient networks. Chances are those with undesirable networks will not be able to offer enough price incentives to get your business, so don't waste your time looking at their quotes. In this transition, we want to keep as many variables constant as possible. If employees can keep their own doctors, the change will not be as drastic.

Step 5: Collecting Plan Designs and Premiums

You now have a shorter list—companies offering group health insurance with decent networks. Of those selling group plans, ask them if they can e-mail you the plan designs for their HDHP plans. If you are offering a dual option, ask to see the PPO plan designs as well. It's likely that they will have a plan that matches up closely to what you currently have.

Most companies will offer between 5 and 20 HDHP plan designs. The features you will want to identify are:

- Individual deductible amount
- Whether family deductibles are embedded
- Co-insurance rate after deductible
- Out-of-pocket maximum (including deductible)
- Prescription co-payments after deductible (if any)
- Preventive benefits offered (if any)
- Whether they bundle their plan with HSAs

Power up Excel and make a list of what you find. Stare at it for a while and see what you learn. You may learn, for instance, that some companies start their deductibles over $2,000. You may find that some companies only offer 100 percent plans. You will probably notice one or two that has every combination of features statistically possible (these were the kids that had to collect every baseball card in the fourth grade).

As you stare at it, you might learn some things
about your own biases. You may already know that
to get this transition going, you had better offer a
starter plan with a low ($1,100–$1,500) deductible.
You can cross off the companies that don't offer
those right now. You may also already know that
you think the preventive benefits will be the key
that sells this strategy in your situation. If so, cross
off the companies that don't offer plans with that
feature attached.

Now you have an even shorter list, and it's time
to collect quotes. There are three ways to ask for
quotes:

- Without employee medical information
- With employee medical information on a
  generic form
- With employee medical information on that
  company's application form

In most situations, quotes without medical information are fiction. They are provided subject to
underwriting and may have a maximum amount
they can travel upward, under your state law. The
only reason to ask for these is that they are easy
and quick to get. You can eliminate providers using
them, but you can't include or select a provider
until you see nonfiction rates. If a rate for a $2,000
deductible HDHP comes in higher than your current $250 deductible PPO, say goodbye to that
provider. If you ask for these rates, you can possibly

narrow down your list even more. It's your call if you want to include this step.

 HSA Hazards

> Quotes from your current insurance company will be guaranteed. You will need to ask them which months you are allowed to change plans. Many carriers will not allow plan changes in the months approaching your renewal date. Some will not allow more than one plan change in a contract year.

Getting quotes with medical information is neither easy nor quick. It involves having your employees fill out medical questionnaires in most cases. Let's say you have three companies on your shortened list. You could pick one application to have your employees fill out, and the other two companies will usually accept that form to give you "prescreened" quotes.

Or you could give your employees all three forms to fill out. This seems like extra work until you realize you'll need to go back to them if you end up selecting a company other than the one whose forms you used initially. Medical questionnaires are not all created equal. One could ask, "Have you smoked in the last year?" while the next one asks, "Do you smoke?" These are not the same question and could change your rate again on final underwriting.

Let me make a quick case for circulating all the forms at once. First it sends a message to the employees that you really are shopping. They don't start making assumptions about what is happening before an actual decision has been made. Second you will get much more accurate (sometimes guaranteed) quotes from each carrier. Again this is your call. Which would be more of a hassle … asking employees to fill out more than one form initially or circulating and collecting forms twice?

Step 6: Selecting a Company and a Plan (or Plans)

As the quotes come in go back to your spreadsheet. (I'm aware that your broker may be giving you a nice comparison, but you need the numbers in a place where you can play with them.) Add three more columns. The first one is for the monthly cost of that plan for your census. If you have asked your current carrier to quote, you will need to manually adjust their quote for the census you are working from.

The second column is for the total HSA deposit. Refer back to Chapter 3 for the maximum yearly contribution amounts and use the following formula:

Number of Employees with Individual Coverage × Maximum Yearly Individual Contribution ÷ 12

+

Number of Employees with Family Coverage × Maximum Yearly Family Contribution ÷ 12

The third column is for the total out-of-pocket expenses not funded by the HSA contribution. You would arrive at this number by the following formula:

Number of Employees with Individual Coverage × (Individual Out-of-Pocket Maximum − Individual Deductible) ÷ 12

+

Number of Employees with Family Coverage × (Family Out-of-Pocket Maximum − Family Deductible) ÷ 12

Now you get to play. First use another column to add the premium to the HSA contribution to get total cash expenditure. Then you could add in the out-of-pocket expenses to that total to get total risk in another column.

Sort your data by the premium. Then sort it by the premium plus the HSA contribution. Then by the total risk. If you really want to have some fun, adjust the premium and the HSA contribution for the tax savings. You're starting to see why you need to have this data in a spreadsheet.

When you sort by the premium cost or the total cash expenditure, you will get lists that are extremely valuable. You can start at either end and do comparisons all the way up or down the list. Look at the amount you can afford based on your compensation calculations we did in Chapter 7. What types of plans are available for that cost?

How do they compare to your current plan? In order to learn this you will have do the calculation of the total risk number you put in your third column. The out-of-pocket maximum plus an average number of office visit co-payments and prescription co-payments will give you what you need.

There are certainly considerations that might have you select a slightly more expensive plan design, but after you have identified networks and browsed at websites, you may find it difficult to justify higher costs for subtle differences. Most of the national insurance companies will tell you that they don't like to compete on cost alone. They prefer to compete on value considerations. One of the values they may offer could be the bundling of the HSA with the HDHP. You can decide if the value of this or other features is worth the extra cost.

Step 7: Determining Cost Sharing and Cash Flow

Once you have found the optimal plan design for your employee group, you have two more decisions to make. 1) How are you going to split the cost in an accounting sense? and 2) When will the HSA deposits be made?

It is helpful to do some analysis of how the new plan will look to a sampling of employees. Take a few employees of different ages, genders, and family size. If you have time, you can do the entire company. See how their paycheck will look with the new plan, if you share the costs with the same percentage or fix their costs or fix your costs. Play with the numbers and put yourself in their position.

HSA Hazards

You may come up with a cost-sharing plan that works for everyone except a couple of stray employees (possibly the young, single males). If you are installing this plan across the board, you may need to make a one-time adjustment to their pay or some other accommodation to help them out. You can't give them a different rate or HSA deposit on an ongoing basis without violating nondiscrimination rules.

If you are offering a dual option, you can be rather creative in how you split the costs to encourage participation in the HDHP. Your splits do not have to be equal at all. In fact, you could have employer money pay the entire premium on the HDHP and make the entire deposit to the HSA and require employee money to "buy up" to the PPO. In many cases, you will need to sweeten the HDHP deal (or sour the PPO deal) to get employees to move.

Step 8: Specific Plan Education

Once you know what you are purchasing, it is back to the blackboard. It has been a few weeks or even months since you had the exploratory conversation with your employees. Start from the beginning and go through how you made this decision and what it will mean to the company and to them. They will ask you in detail every calculation and how it will affect them. If you know in advance that you have a couple of people who will be markedly worse off, talk to them privately first so they don't monopolize the meeting.

Come to the meeting with a detailed explanation of the plan they currently have and the plan you are moving to or offering them as an option. Calculate the out-of-pocket risk on their current plan so they can see that what they are moving to is better. Calculate their tax savings and do some projections on their HSA balances and future year premium savings. Each employee will lock onto what makes sense to him or her.

Be very prepared to discuss the "gap financing" method (see Chapter 8) you have selected. Do this early in the meeting as it is the major obstacle to overcome.

If you are also changing insurance companies, have a company representative end the meeting with how to deal with that company. They will be eager to speak about those "value" items they believe sell their product. Let them do it. It makes them happy.

Step 9: Enrolling Employees in HDHPs and Opening HSAs

If you had the employees fill out all the applications in advance and less than 90 days has passed, you won't need new applications from most people. There will be some who, after hearing all the education pieces, are changing their minds. They now want on or off the plan. They might want to drop or add a dependent. They will need to fill out new applications. Give people a firm deadline for these changes. After that deadline changes will take effect the following month, but new enrollees would need to wait until the next open enrollment period.

 HSA Hazards

Make sure employees know that if they are not currently on the health plan in force, the insurer may add a pre-existing conditions clause to their new policy. Under this clause, conditions that have had treatment or a diagnosis in the last six months would not be covered for the first year. Under HIPAA (Health Insurance Portability and Accountability Act of 1996) anyone covered on your current plan would not have this clause.

Step 10: Follow-Up Support/Education

The adoption of an HDHP/HSA plan will require ongoing support for the first year. Assign someone in the company to collect questions and seek out answers. The insurance company customer support line and your broker should be a first line of resources. You might seek assistance from your company's accountant as well to coach employees through the tax questions they may have. Consider distributing a short education piece around the time that W-2's are issued.

You may want to keep the troublemaker committee in place to work through some of the transitional issues. If you have followed the ten steps outlined in this chapter, you will have fewer issues than most employers. Your employees will have a solid plan that they value. They will understand how it works and why it is good for the company and for them.

It will be an ongoing challenge to educate new employees as they join your company. Put together the best resources you found as you moved through this process and develop an education tool while it is fresh in your mind. You might also assign mentors to new employees.

The Least You Need to Know

- The process to convert to an HDHP/HSA strategy takes three to six months and needs strong leadership.
- Early employee awareness and education can help guide several decisions that need to be made along the way.
- Evaluate insurance companies by eliminating those that have weak networks and unacceptable plan designs early in the process.
- Compare and select plans by doing a variety of financial analysis calculations separate from those offered by your broker.

10

Personal Financial Planning Strategies

In This Chapter

- Fitting your HSA into your financial plan
- Guiding your employees with HSA strategies
- Long-term investment and tax decisions

So you've got this new gadget, an HSA. Now what do you do with it? Fund it to the max? Put in only money you need for your current expenses? Never take a penny out? Or only keep $5 in it? As far as I can tell it really doesn't matter. You can only make good and better decisions regarding this account. So you have some time to figure it out.

Good Decisions and Better Decisions

Start with one strategy, knowing that you can switch if your situation changes. These accounts are so flexible that your only problem will be that you have too many choices. Let's go through some of the strategies you could adopt and see which might fit your situation. As you are reading, also think about which strategies your employees may favor so you will be ready to help field their questions.

The Retirement Fund

In this strategy, your goal is to qualify to put the most money possible into your HSA each year by buying an HDHP with a deductible at or above that year's maximum deposit. Then you don't withdraw any money, even if you have qualifying expenses. The goal of this strategy is to accumulate tax-free deposits and earnings in anticipation of higher medical costs during retirement. This account would be tapped each year of retirement equal to the amount of unreimbursed medical expenses during that year.

In this strategy, the money deposited and its earnings could never incur income tax. This fund becomes the foundation of your retirement planning. Unlike other tax-deferred accounts, such as IRAs and 401(k)s, the withdrawals might not be taxed. To find the cash to afford this strategy, you would probably be reassigning money already targeted for retirement savings. It is unlikely that the premium savings from the higher deductible HDHPs would result in enough cash to make the maximum deposit out of that cash flow. If you have after-tax investments, you can move money from them each year. If all of your retirement money is going into tax-deferred vehicles, you will still gain a tax advantage by redirecting as much as possible each year into the HSA.

Unfortunately you cannot roll over funds already tax-deferred in IRAs, 401(k)s, and other retirement vehicles into HSAs. But because these funds are often available without penalty at age 59½ you can make withdrawals and pay your income tax. Up to age 64, you could then deposit the money into your HSA, taking a deduction in the same year. You are limited to the amount of the annual maximum HSA contribution. Remember that this amount is increased by the catch-up amount allowed between age 55 and 64.

Because the account is targeted from its inception as a long-term investment, the *asset allocation* of the investment should reflect that decision. You would be shopping for HSA fiduciaries that offer a full range of risk/return options in their investment vehicles. You would use the same asset allocation plan that you are comfortable with in your current retirement plan.

Case Study: David and Carol are married and both 50 years old. They have owned a wallpaper whole-sale company for 20 years. Like many small business owners, they didn't take much income for themselves in the first few years and likewise got a late start on their retirement savings. They hope to be able to sell the business in about 15 years to fund most of their retirement goals. They are also funding other investments to round out their plan.

Word Doctor _____

Asset allocation is the process of deciding how to divide up your money into investments that carry different risks, different liquidity, and different returns. You might see an investor's asset allocation stated as 15 percent cash, 25 percent short-term bonds, 20 percent large company stock, 20 percent small company stock, and 20 percent international stock.

They have purchased an HDHP with a $6,000 family deductible, reducing their premiums by $4,000 per year. They plan to use the premium savings to pay any out-of-pocket expenses and bank the rest in a short-term regular savings account, in case they have a hospitalization. They will keep records of their expenses because these costs can be withdrawn from their HSA at any time in the future.

They currently invest $20,000 each year into long-term tax-deferred investments. They plan to redirect $5,450 during 2006 (the maximum deposit allowed) into their HSA. They will increase their deposit each year, as the maximum is indexed upward. If we assume the index might be 2 percent each year, they will have to raise the deductible on their HDHP in year seven (the year when the indexing will raise the maximum deposit above their deductible). Otherwise they would be limited to depositing the $6,000 deductible amount. They also plan to make the additional $1,000 contribution allowed for each of them from age 55 to 64. This will total approximately $110,000 of deposits resulting in around $150,000 in the account (assuming a 4 percent inflation adjusted return).

At age 65, they can no longer deposit to the HSA. If they have not yet sold the business, they can redirect their HSA deposit back to other retirement vehicles. If they have sold the business, they can begin their withdrawal strategy. Just like any retirement withdrawal strategy, they will spend money that has already been taxed first. Next they will spend down their HSA funds, leaving any investments still waiting to be taxed for last or until they are forced to make withdrawals under the tax laws.

Remember all those records of qualified expenses they have been keeping for 15 years? They totaled $25,000. David and Carol will take money out of their HSA to "reimburse" themselves for those expenses. There will be no tax on these withdrawals, even if they didn't buy one aspirin that year. They will only take what they need for living expenses, however, because they will want to leave as much in the account as they can to continue to grow income tax-free. There is no penalty for leaving money in an HSA too long.

Beyond the $25,000, they can also reimburse themselves for their current unreimbursed expenses,

Medicare Part B and D premiums, long-term care insurance premiums, dental and vision expenses, and over-the-counter medications. Each year they will add up what they have incurred and make a withdrawal (or withdrawals).

In the fortunate event that they live out their retirement in relatively good health and rarely need to spend money on qualified medical expenses, they can still take out the money. After age 65, there is no excise tax (the 10 percent penalty) on withdrawals not used for qualified expenses. So in essence, after age 65, the HSA withdrawals are treated the same as withdrawals from an IRA or 401(k).

In this example, David and Carol have gained a tax benefit from making withdrawals from the tax-advantaged HSA over the tax-deferred retirement vehicles they were currently funding. If we assume that they would select similar, if not the same, underlying investments, then they have gained the tax on the $150,000 balance that their HSA realized by age 65 plus whatever it earns after their retirement date. Depending upon how well their other investments have done, and how they are being paid for their business, this could mean from $10,000 to $75,000 in tax savings.

At the same time they are creating this tax savings, they are also accumulating additional after-tax savings from the $4,000 they have saved on the premium each year. After medical expenses, they were able to put away another $40,000 toward retirement.

Insurance Insights

Unless you name your spouse as the beneficiary of your HSA, the account loses its tax status as an HSA when you die. Its fair market value becomes taxable to the beneficiary in the year you die. If you leave it to your spouse, it becomes his or her HSA.

This strategy merely involves making decisions similar to what you might already be doing to prepare for retirement and folding the new tax advantages of the HSA into those tactics. Your cash flow looks exactly the same. The same amount would be budgeted for retirement savings. And you are spending the same amount for your short-term health-care needs when you add together your new lower premium for the HDHP and your after-tax savings for current medical expenses.

The Emergency Fund

In the Retirement Fund strategy above, there was no thought that the HSA funds would be used prior to retirement for emergency purposes. The assumption in the case of David and Carol was that their short-term saving was safely elsewhere, invested in liquid, less risky, after-tax vehicles. And we know that they had medical emergencies already planned for.

But what if they had a nonmedical family emergency that needed cash? They can make nontaxable withdrawals from their HSA at any time, up to the amount of the incurred medical expenses. They can also make taxable withdrawals at any time. These features of the HSA make it a possible fallback emergency fund.

Premium Advice

I know you don't stay awake at night thinking up ways to make it easier for your employees to quit, but even for loyal employees having an HSA as an emergency fund can feel like a tremendous benefit, especially if they have children. If you have a layoff or they quit and want to remain on your policy through COBRA, they can use their HSA funds to pay these premiums.

This strategy differs slightly from the first strategy in that you would need a different asset allocation model. Instead of jumping right into a long-term allocation, you would want to weight it more toward a short-term allocation until you have built up most of the emergency fund you would need. The problem with long-term allocations is that the cycles of the investments might be too volatile. If their value is low at the exact moment you have an emergency you would take a loss when withdrawing the funds you need.

Self-Insurance

Back to basics here, for just a second. Let's pretend
you lease a car and the leasing company makes you
buy collision insurance on it. Reasonable request.
But they make you buy a $250 deductible. You
explain to them that you have $1,000 in the bank
that you will use to fix the car if you wreck it, so
you only need a $1,000 deductible on the policy.
The premium is much lower and it makes sense to
you. They say, "No." What they are afraid of is
this: you will no longer have the $1,000 when the
day comes to fix the car.

What you were proposing was a form of self-
insurance. You insure the first $1,000. The insur-
ance company insures the remainder of the value
of the car. You could then take the savings in your
premium and increase that $1,000 to $2,000 over
some period of time. Now you need a $2,000
deductible and you enjoy an even lower premium.
At the same time, the value of the car is decreasing.
You continue this strategy until the day when the
value of the car is less than the balance in the savings account. You drop the coverage.

Now you wreck the car, total it; it's gone forever.
You happily go down to your bank, get out your
money and go get another car. Or do you? Doesn't
it bother you just a little bit that the insurance
company didn't have to write a check? It might and
if it does, get over it. This is why you are insurance
poor. You haven't embraced the wonderful concept
of self-insurance.

HSAs give you a wonderful format to practice this approach. You start with a lower, say $1,500 deductible. The first two years you save that amount and don't withdraw it. You pay your medical expenses with other funds. Now you have $3,000 in the bank and a policy with a $1,500 deductible. You can raise the deductible.

Premium Advice

You can offer a dual option for employees who are using the self-insurance strategy. They can move up to a higher deductible eventually. The lower deductible stays an option for those not accumulating cash and those new to your company.

The highest deductible you can currently have is $5,250 for an individual and $10,500 for a family. How can you tell when you're ready to move up? A safe formula would be when you have the new deductible in your account. But you could move before then, knowing that you will be able to deposit even more after you raise the deductible.

Employees seem to like this approach in concept, but they quickly figure out that the future decreases in premiums may not add up to all that much for them. We are a country of very poor savers, and savings is not where we automatically start when thinking about our financial security. Moving through this concept with your employees usually sounds more like this message:

> We know that insurance rates will continue to rise at some rate. Putting ourselves in the position of needing less insurance in the future will give us more control over our paychecks.

Notice you didn't use the word savings anywhere in there!

The self-insurance strategy demands a very short-term asset allocation approach. You are planning to be ready at a moment's notice for any medical expenses that you incur, while trying to build a larger balance that will support a higher deductible on your HDHP. Because the deductible cannot rise beyond the $5,250/$10,500 limit and still qualify you to make tax-deductible deposits, at some point you will have more money than you need to cover the deductible. Then you could separate out the short-term and long-term money into different investment strategies.

The Insurance Supplement

The difference between this strategy and self-insurance is that you don't start with the goal of accumulating a higher and higher balance to be able to raise your deductible. Instead you start with the notion that you are going to pay all of your insured medical expenses out of this account that are not paid by the insurance company. It feels like a secondary insurance policy to you because the claims go to your insurance company and if they are not paid, you have them take the money from this account or you take it out yourself and pay the bill. If you are lucky enough to have a good year and you find yourself with a high balance at the end of the year, then you make the decision to raise your deductible. But you are not devastated if it has to remain the same.

This strategy assumes that you begin each year with a set schedule for deposits, prior to knowing what your expenses will be. You might even make the full deposit early in the year for the convenience of knowing the money is already there and all expenses that apply to the deductible will be covered.

Premium Advice

Employees will begin at the insurance-supplement strategy. It is the first use of the account they understand because it is the way that most informational material is written. They will calculate the benefits of the HDHP/HSA approach using this strategy. They will answer the question of whether they can pay their medical expenses when incurred. Some will move on to other strategies and some won't.

If you end the year with unused deposits, you will reduce your contribution during the following year to total your maximum risk for the next year.

Example: Josh has a $1,100 deductible 100 percent HDHP. His employer contributes $50 per month to his HSA. The first year he decides to contribute the other $41.67 per month allowed. At the end of the first year, he has a balance in his account of $850 because he only had a check-up and one sinus infection during the year. His employer will continue to make the $50 deposit each month during the second year, so Josh stops his voluntary contribution. He knows that even if he has a horrible year and lands in the hospital, he'll end the year with $350 in his account after all his medical bills are paid.

This is a short-term, budget centered strategy. No investment decisions would need to be made because the goal is to use the money for expenses. If most of the employees are happy with this mindset, then the choice of a fiduciary is solely based on who has the cheapest checking account fees.

The Ancillary Insurance

This is the strategy that actually excites employees the most and comes closest to being a bad decision, at least in the first year. But if handled right, it can be a good decision. The difference between this strategy and the insurance-supplement strategy is that you use HSA funds to pay for additional items that will not apply to the HDHP deductible.

Refer again to the list of qualified expenses that can be withdrawn tax-free from an HSA in Appendix B. There are a lot of items that are not covered by the HDHP. The main categories are dental/vision care, over-the-counter medications, and insurance premiums. We can add to the list all legitimate medical expenses incurred at non-network providers and all expenses that have exceeded any internal limits on the policy (e.g., mental health visits).

This is where the HSA rules can complicate our management of the account. Let's look at an example:

Case Study: Kari works for a design firm that offers a dual option health-insurance package. She chose the $2,000 deductible 80 percent HDHP. Her employer is depositing half of the deductible into her HSA and she chose to deposit an additional $30 per month. She is relatively healthy and doesn't expect to use $1,360 for medical expenses in a normal year.

Her employer offers a voluntary dental program that she feels is too expensive just to pay for her routine exams, so she opted out of that benefit. She decides to use money from her HSA to pay for her dental visits that totaled $320 for the year. She also had her yearly check-up which ran $200. Her HSA balance in December was $840.

On Christmas Eve, she slipped on some ice on her brother's porch and spent the rest of the night in the emergency room with a broken arm. After the surgery to insert pins, the bill for all the services she received came to $4,500.

She had already met $200 of her $2,000 deductible, so she would be responsible for the remaining $1,800. On her 80 percent plan she would be responsible for 20 percent of the amount over $2,000. This comes to $500 (20 percent of $2,500). Her share of the broken arm came to $2,300. She is not too upset because her employer had deposited $1,000 and she saved at least another $1,300 in premiums this year, moving to the HSA.

The challenge is that she used $320 out of her HSA for her dental expenses, so that money isn't there to help pay for the broken arm. She knew she was taking that risk when she withdrew the money. She looked at it this way: she was able to tax-deduct her dental expenses if she didn't need the money for her deductible. Since she broke her arm and did need the money, the $320 she'll have to kick in from after-tax money is what she would have paid to the dentist in the first place. She ends up the same.

Kari used the money for her dental expenses knowing that she was dipping into money she might need later. This is the important aspect of this strategy. If she has the money elsewhere or can afford the $320 out of cash flow in any given month, she'll be fine. The employees who are taking the money from their HSAs because they can't afford to see the dentist are the ones who will be at risk.

A conservative approach to this strategy would be to only use the HSA money throughout the first year for items that do apply to the deductible. At the end of the year, if there are funds left unused, then reimburse yourself for those qualified expenses you incurred during the year. Or let them ride and spend them on next year's expenses.

The Tax Deduction

Some people don't like to part with their cash until the last possible second. HSAs offer a strategy for these folks, too. This strategy is a little like giving your teenagers money. They already know exactly what they want it for and they don't have it for long.

Remember that you can deposit money into an HSA up to April 15 of the year following the tax year when you were covered by the HDHP. And remember that you can withdraw funds for expenses incurred anytime in the past when the HSA was open. This strategy would have you paying your expenses throughout the year with some other account and saving the receipts. You could even use a cash-back credit card to make a little cash. After December 31, anytime you get around to it, up until April 15, you add up all the receipts and you make a deposit to your HSA for that amount. Then you write a check or make a cash withdrawal for the same amount. (If it's a large amount, the bank may make you wait a few days for the funds to clear). That's it. You get to deduct the deposit from your taxable income. The withdrawal will not be taxed because you were reimbursing yourself for qualified expenses.

HSA Hazards

If you leave your HSA to your estate, the value will be added to your final income tax return.

This is the strategy for those who don't want to manage a second account. It also comes in handy when cash is tight. Maybe you are trying to retire some debt that would pay you a much higher return than even the tax-free savings in an HSA. You reduce your insurance costs by moving to an HDHP and hold back the money you save for your out-of-pocket expenses. If you have qualified medical expenses, you can run them through the HSA to realize the tax savings. If you have no expenses, you can use the money to retire the debt.

The account that works the best for this strategy is one without a monthly maintenance fee, but makes it up with huge transaction fees. You'd only have two transactions a year. You don't care. There will never be a balance, so there will never be a need to decide where to invest it.

The Least You Need to Know

- HSAs are one of the most powerful and flexible savings vehicles we have to plan for our financial security.
- You can integrate an HSA into your retirement planning, increasing the amount

available to you at retirement without investing any additional today because of the tax savings.

- You can also position your HSA to be available during emergencies, for example, helping with the cost of COBRA premiums.

- The basic strategies of using the account to reduce your need for low deductible insurance coverage and saving taxes on current medical expenses are the primary strategies that most people begin with.

Comparing and Combining HSAs with FSAs and HRAs

In This Chapter

- The basic features of FSAs (Flexible Spending Accounts)
- A comparison of HSAs with HRAs (Health Reimbursement Arrangements)
- How to combine HSAs with HRAs and FSAs

As I've wandered around in the last year and a half telling strangers that my job involves working with HSAs, I often get the response, "Oh, yeah, we have that at work." "I bet you don't," I would reply, and then the long explanation would begin.

When people first hear the term Health Savings Account, their minds go to Flexible Spending Accounts, which are neither flexible nor accounts, it turns out, when compared to HSAs. FSAs are part of the Section 125 (Cafeteria Plan) tax rules that allow employees a tax deduction for certain insurance premiums, uncovered medical expenses, and dependent care expenses.

Flexible Spending Accounts

An employee can ask for a pre-tax payroll deduction that sends money to an administrator, who in turn sends it back to them when they submit receipts for qualifying expenses. The list of qualifying medical expenses is, coincidentally, the same list the government used to describe qualifying medical expenses for HSA withdrawals (in Appendix B).

The employer sets the limit for the maximum an employee can ask to be withheld, and for good reason. If an employee asks for 10 dollars per week to be withheld ($520 per year), the employer is on the hook for the entire $520 during the first month. In exchange for taking this risk, the employer receives the unused remainder left in each employee's account at the end of the year.

These plans are normally installed by larger companies that have the cash flow to absorb the potential extra expenses early in the year. They do carry administrative expenses, which are normally born by the employer. Employers are allowed to contribute but often don't. Employees who participate will try to calculate their expected expenses during the coming year so they won't lose their deposits at the end of the year. Vendors, such as opticians, will have sales in December, knowing that people may have FSA funds they are about to lose.

Combining HSAs and FSAs

Combining HSAs and FSAs is a little like owning both a cat and dog. If they grow up together, they get along. If they are both adults when they meet, one of them is gonna get hurt.

The key issue is this: in order to qualify to make contributions to an HSA, you may not have health coverage that pays for any medical expenses before $1,050. If the FSA is set up to reimburse for those early expenses, before the HDHP deductible is met, you are breaking the rule. You would then be disqualified from making tax-free deposits to the HSA.

If you already have an FSA, you can modify it to only pay expenses after the deductible (just like getting the cat declawed). It can also pay expenses not covered by the health plan, such as dental and vision. This is a reasonable solution for those companies that have come to love their FSA, but be prepared for an onslaught of questions and confusion. You would be wise, in this situation, to have your FSA administrator also manage the HSA funding. You should find a knowledgeable representative to whom you can pass along these questions.

 Premium Advice

Since business owners cannot participate in the Flexible Spending Account tax benefits, many are opting for HSAs while their employees continue to participate in FSAs.

Combining HDHPs and FSAs

It is perfectly fine to have an HDHP and an FSA together. If you never open HSAs, there are no rules to be broken. From your perspective, this may be the perfect solution to ease into an HDHP. If you already have an FSA operating and you switch from a PPO to an HDHP, employees could use their premium savings to increase their deposits to the FSA to cover the higher deductible. Cash-flow problems early in the year would disappear because you are immediately responsible for their entire yearly contribution.

Insurance Insights

Each employee must file an 8889 with his or her 1040 tax return if they had any activity in or out of their HSA during the tax year. There is no separate tax form required for employees contributing to a Flexible Spending Account.

Even though they aren't spending any more money up front, employees might stand to lose their deposits at the end of the year if they have a year with low claims. Additionally, the other benefits of the HSA would not be realized. The employees would not own the account and could not accumulate money in it past the end of the plan year. Rules were relaxed recently to allow them a little more time to file claims, but any balance remaining would still disappear at some point. A nice transition would be to pick a January 1st date in the next year or two and have each employee open an HSA to begin to receive deposits on that date. You could phase out the FSA or leave it in place to fund post-deductible and ancillary expenses.

Health Reimbursement Arrangements

Imagine an HDHP/HSA setup where the HDHP had no rules about what type of plan you choose and the HSA money was never owned by the employee. You're getting close to a Health Reimbursement Arrangement (HRA).

An HRA is a promise to pay, usually combined with a slightly higher deductible plan, but not necessarily. The HRA does not have to be a separately funded account. The money can stay in your general operating account. How and what you promise to pay is written out in a plan design document that you have tremendous control over. This is an employer-centric strategy that can save premiums on your health plan, while leaving your employees with the same coverage.

Premium Advice _____

> Remember that HRAs do not usually accumulate money that employees could use toward insurance premiums for policies such as COBRA coverage and Long-Term Care insurance.

HRAs share a lot of similarities with the self-insurance strategy I described in Chapter 10. With the HSA Self-Insurance Strategy, each employee is building his or her own reserve toward a higher deductible. Larger employers enter into official self-insured plans, where only amounts over $10,000 or more are covered by the insurance company. HRAs fall somewhere in between these two approaches.

Case Study: Joe runs a lawn care company with 30 employees. They are mostly young and many are recent immigrants. Most of them do not have bank accounts. They cash their weekly paycheck at the check-cashing company, buy money orders for their few bills, and spend the rest. When they need medical care, they rely heavily on the $15 co-payment Joe's plan provides. They don't know or care that they have a $250 deductible because they can't afford it anyway. They would make payments to the hospital if they ever needed surgery. They split the premium with Joe through a weekly payroll deduction and many are dropping coverage after this year's premium increase.

Joe knows that with the young and active work-force, they are not likely to experience high claims. Any accidents would be covered by workers' compensation, and his employees ignore most minor illnesses until they go away. He decides to reduce his premiums by 30 percent and move to a $2,000 deductible plan, increasing to a $20 co-payment for office visits and adding a $500 limited drug benefit. This reduces the premium back to a level where the workers can afford to pay half and gives him $20,000 cash to fund an HRA.

With $20,000, 10 of his employees could use their entire $2,000 deductibles and Joe would be no worse off than he was under his old plan. If only nine of them use it, he is better off. He doesn't have to dedicate the money to this use in advance. Each employee would submit claims to him (or his administrator) after the insurance company processes them. He does have a similar risk to the FSA plans in that it is possible that claims could be clustered early in the year. And there is the possibility that more than 10 employees could use their deductibles.

He can also write his HRA document to provide other benefits. He could, for instance, pay the additional $5 co-payment for office visits. He could pay for prescriptions after the $500 benefit has been exhausted. He could pay for dental and vision services up to any amount he chooses. He can write the plan however he feels his employees would be the most appreciative. He can also share the costs with his employees. For instance, he could ask them to continue to pay the first $250 of the deductible and the HRA could pay the remaining $1,750.

Some plan designs actually provide each employee with an accounting (not an account) of how much money they have accumulated to spend in their HRA. Instead of promising a benefit (say a $2,000 deductible), they accrue amounts on a monthly basis toward approved expenses. This feels more like an HSA to the employee, where they need to budget their withdrawals. Advocates of this approach claim it adds the "consumer directed" feel to the account. Unlike with HSAs, the employee never owns the money in HRAs and can't take it with them, so it seems that the consumer effect would be much less than with an HSA.

Combining HRAs and HSAs

Once again, that sticky little rule gets in our way: you can't have any benefit, policy plan, or agreement that pays before you reach your de-ductible. A lot of quick thinking brokers and employers thought it would be nifty to have an HRA that pays that gap in the first year between the deductible and what you may deposit to an HSA, if you begin the plan after January 1st.

You can't have HRAs and HSAs in place at the same time for this purpose, however.

HRAs do provide a possible solution for the first year cash-flow problems of HSAs. You could install a qualified HDHP with the intention of having employees open HSAs in January. Until then you could put an HRA document into plan, promising them reimbursement for expenses up to their deductibles. When the HSAs are opened, the HRA goes away. This eases the transition to the HDHP/HSA strategy.

Just like the limited FSAs we discussed earlier in this chapter, you can have an HRA that will pay for expenses after the deductible and those not covered by the health plan. Some employers are now considering a simpler approach to dental insurance by installing an HRA, either with a capped amount per year (like the pun?) or a stated list of services that are covered.

HRAs are a wonderful solution to a situation where you find the almost perfect plan design with a great rate but something is missing. Maybe, this plan limits services for chiropractic care and you have a number of employees who really value that care. You could install an HRA to reimburse for chiropractic care not reimbursed by the health plan. Large companies do this kind of tweaking all the time when designing their own self-insured plans. With HRAs it is possible to have that type of flexibility as a small business.

Insurance Insights

Even though it is difficult to offer HRA and HSA plans together to your employees, it is very easy to offer them a choice between the two. Many business owners and managers will pick the HSA option while other staff will likely pick the HRA option. This is the best of both worlds.

Shopping for FSAs and HRAs

If either the FSA or HRA options look interesting to you, your next step should be to start talking to folks who can handle them for you. You have several options for both. Neither of these plans is insured, meaning that you are not pooling risk with any other employers so you don't need an insurance company to pool that risk. You have the option of administering them yourself, using a third party administrator, or asking an insurance company to administer them.

Self-Administered Plans

The first option you have is to administer your FSA or HRA yourself. You will need a plan document that you would normally have an attorney or accountant create for you that outlines what you want the plan to do.

Then you would communicate to your employees what their benefits, rights, and responsibilities are under the plan. They would enroll and select any options you offer them, such as the contribution amount to an FSA. The employees would submit bills or explanations of benefits to you as they had expenses to be reimbursed. You would pay them as you would reimburse them for any expense.

This sounds like no big deal to some employers and a lot of work to others. If you have a simple plan and a limited number of times you cut checks (say, once a month) it might not be a lot of work. Keep in mind that you will be privy to private health information that you will need to protect under the HIPAA privacy rules, which adds another level of complexity to the process.

If you are installing an HRA for a limited time to buy time until you open HSA accounts, doing it yourself may make sense. You would minimize the transitional issues by not forcing your employees to get used to another new company.

One of the problems with administering it yourself is the possibility that you pay for an expense not defined by the plan. Either by accident or coercion, you might step over the line that defines what is reimbursable. Professional administrators have more experience determining these boundaries and denying claims when appropriate.

Accountants, Bookkeepers, and Payroll Services

The accounting and reporting functions of these plans can be handled by anyone who regularly does your other accounting functions. The money would remain in your account and your accountant would help you by deciding which payments need to go out and creating reports of these payments.

They may or may not have the experience to help you create your plan design and mediate any disputes over claim decisions. They would give you the distance needed to help with confidentiality issues and reduce any coercion you might feel from certain employees.

Payroll services are also getting into this act. Many now offer FSA and HRA reimbursement services. They are building on their relationships with employers around the country and adding these services to their list of options.

Third Party Administrator

Get ready, here comes another three-letter acronym: TPA. These firms are like mini-insurance companies. Some of them used to be insurance companies and gave up the risk-pooling part of the job. Now they push around paper and money, hopefully in the right directions, and help companies calculate estimated costs on self-insured plans. They do need to be licensed with your state's insurance department so you can find them through the phone numbers in Appendix E.

Many of them are very small and very customer friendly. You can get to know their staff and stop by their office when you want to chat. Some operate across several states or nationally. The larger they are, the more automation they can offer you. The largest ones will have web-based services that your employees can access.

They will help you design your plans, conduct employee education sessions, handle all the payments from the plan and create any year-end reports you might need. The fees are usually charged by the service or by the person per month. They should be able to tell you up front what most of the fees will be, so you can decide if it is worth the money to farm this out.

Insurance Companies

Insurance companies have been slow to offer these products to companies with fewer than 100 employees. They just don't find the profit margin they need in groups smaller than that. If you have more than 100 employees or you find one that will service smaller employers, there are some advantages.

Your employees already know the company. The customer service might be streamlined so a problem on either side of the claim could be handled with one phone call.

They are likely to offer automatic claim forwarding (the same concept we discussed with HSA accounts). If an employee has an insurance plan and an HRA with the same insurance company, both claims would be paid before they received the explanation of benefits. This is much easier than receiving the insurance company's report and forwarding it on to the TPA or accountant handling the HRA. Both payments to the vendor would come from the insurance company, instead of one coming from the employee.

Making a Change

The good news is that there are lots of options and plan designs. We have come a long way since double-digit rate increases began chipping away at your bottom line. You no longer need to feel trapped by the renewal letters happily mailed to you each year. The industry, with a little help from our friends in Washington, has responded to the desperation felt by employers everywhere.

Which of their responses works best for you is your call. I hope I've opened up some possibilities for you as you explored the many ways to structure HSAs. And given you even more to think about as you explore FSAs and HRAs.

In the short year and a half (at this writing) that HSAs have been in existence, the industry has changed its offerings dozens of times. Every company is positioning and repositioning to be stronger in the market, but they are listening to you. Where you take your insurance dollars this year will be a loud vote for what they need to offer. Consumer-driven health care not only refers to the control that consumers will take over their own health; it also refers to the control that they will take over the insurance companies' marketing and product plans.

Thank you for the opportunity to share this exciting new direction in health insurance with you. I look forward to even more creative and adventurous moves from the industry and Congress in the near future. By the next writing of this book, I hope to include solutions that you and your employees have participated in developing. Whatever change you make, let everyone know what is working and what isn't. Everyone will benefit from your experience.

The Least You Need to Know

- Flexible Spending Accounts (FSAs) are well-known to many employees of larger companies and are often confused with Health Savings Accounts at first.

- Health Reimbursement Arrangements (HRAs) are relatively new and allow the employer to retain ownership of cash targeted for deductibles and other reimbursements.

- The combination of either an FSA or HRA with an HSA can jeopardize the tax status of the HSA and should be done very carefully.

- You can install and administer an FSA or HRA yourself; with the help of your accountant or payroll service; or through a third-party administrator or an insurance company.

Glossary

accident insurance   Health insurance policy that covers expenses incurred due to an accident.

acute care   Health treatment given for short-term, often serious medical conditions.

accelerated (or catch-up) contributions
Additional tax-deferred deposits to Health Savings Accounts allowed between the ages of 55 and 64. In 2005—$600; 2006—$700; 2007—$800; 2008—$900; 2009—$1,000.

after-tax contributions   Deposits made to a Health Savings Accounts through payroll deduction arrangements, using money already taxed by the federal, state, and local governments. A deduction can be taken when filing federal taxes for these deposits.

after-tax premiums   Insurance premiums paid through payroll deduction arrangements using money already taxed by the federal, state, and local governments.

allocation   The manner in which a deposit is divided among investment options.

annual (or open) enrollment   The month (or two) each year that an employer may add participants to a group insurance plan.

appreciation   The increase in an asset's (or investment's) value over time due to market conditions or retained earnings.

asset   A tangible or intangible item that can be bought or sold.

balance billing   The practice of medical providers who charge the patient the amounts beyond what is paid by the insurance coverage.

before-tax contributions   Deposits made to a Health Savings Accounts through payroll deduction arrangements, using money not taxed by the federal, state, and local governments. A deduction cannot be taken when filing federal taxes for these deposits.

before-tax premiums   Insurance premiums paid through payroll deduction arrangements using money not taxed by the federal, state, and local governments.

beneficiary   Person or persons named by the Health Savings Account holder to receive the balance in the account on his or her death.

bond   An investment choice for Health Savings Accounts that is a debt owed by the issuing company (or government) to the investor, paying a regular, stated interest rate.

brand name drug   A drug, usually patented, available from one pharmaceutical manufacturer.

cafeteria plan   A set of insurance options that employees may select from, usually using pre-tax dollars to purchase through payroll deduction.

calendar year deductible   The amount of medical services a policyholder must incur before benefits are paid by the insurance company, which starts over every January 1.

carryover deductible   A calendar year deductible that continues to accrue even though a policy-holder has changed plans or carriers during the year.

claim   A statement requesting payment or reim-bursement for stated services provided by a medical professional or facility on behalf of an insured patient.

claim form   The form used by a specific insur-ance company to provide details of medical services rendered.

claimant   The insured individual who has received medical services and is requesting reim-bursement or payment.

COBRA   Referring to the provisions of the Con-solidated Omnibus Budget Reconciliation Act of 1985 (as amended). Often used as a noun or adjective (e.g., COBRA benefits) to describe con-tinuation of coverage of a group health plan after separation of employment.

co-insurance The split defined in a health-insurance policy that divides costs between the insured and the health-insurance company, usually after a deductible is met, and prior to an out-of-pocket maximum being met. (e.g., 80 percent insurance company, 20 percent insured).

common stock A portion of ownership in a public or private corporation, entitled to participate in the profits of the corporation through declared dividends.

compound interest Income from an investment calculated as a percentage of the current balance of the investment, including previous interest earned.

consumer driven health plan (CDHP) A variety of health-insurance plans that encourage consumer participation in health-care selection and cost management through various means, including higher deductibles and other cost sharing methods.

consumer price index (CPI) A number (stated as a percentage) generated by the federal government that approximates inflation by measuring the rise in prices of a fixed set of goods and services.

coordination of benefits The order that benefits are paid when an insured is covered by more than one health insurance policy.

co-payment A flat fee paid for a medical service, such as a visit to a physician or a supply of a prescribed drug, after which the insurance company pays the rest of the cost.

covered dependent   A person, such as a spouse or child, who is insured on an employee's group health coverage.

covered expenses   The medical services a contract for health insurance will reimburse for the cost of receiving.

covered person   All insured individuals, both employees and dependents, on a group health plan.

critical care   Medical services provided to patients who are severely ill, often in intensive care or emergency room facilities.

daily benefit   Fixed amount paid on hospitalization policies for each day in the hospital, rather than a percentage of services charged.

deductible   The amount the insured is required to pay prior to certain benefits beginning.

dental plan   An insurance contract that reimburses for stated dental care expenses.

dependent care Flexible Spending Account (FSA)   An employer sponsored pre-tax payroll deduction plan to pay for dependent care expenses.

diagnostic services   Medical services to discover the presence or cause of a condition or disease.

diversification   Investing assets in a variety of investments with differing risks and returns.

elective care   Medical services that have no specific time constraints and can be scheduled at the convenience of the patient or provider.

eligibility period   The time during which an employee is permitted to elect coverage in a group plan.

eligible dependent   Persons defined by the plan who may elect coverage because of their relationship to the employee (e.g., spouse, disabled adult child, etc.).

eligible employee   Person employed by the company that purchases the group insurance plan who meets criteria specified by law or the plan (e.g., full-time, salaried, permanent, etc.).

eligible expenses   Medical care costs that are defined by the plan to be reimbursable when incurred by the insured.

embedded deductible   *See* family deductible (embedded).

emergency care   Medical services received in the event of a sudden, critical health problem.

EOB   Referring to Explanation of Benefits, a document provided by an insurance company to the provider and the insured in response to a claim, detailing the eligible expenses and reimbursements to be paid.

ERISA   Referring to the provisions of the Employee Retirement Income Security Act of 1974, as amended, that regulates most of the employee benefit plans in effect in the United States.

evidence of insurability   Documents and data requested by an insurance company to qualify to enter into an insurance contract.

exclusion   A type of expense named by an insurance policy as specifically not reimbursable.

excise tax   The additional percentage imposed by the Internal Revenue Service as a penalty when depositing or withdrawing amounts from Health Savings Accounts over the stated limits.

family deductible (embedded)   A combination of two or more individual deductibles that, when met, waives the individual deductibles for all other family members.

family deductible (nonembedded or aggregate) A deductible met by the combined expenses of all family members.

fixed matching contributions   A set amount that an employer contributes to an employee's Health Savings Account, based on an employee contribution of the same amount.

Flexible Spending Account (FSA)   An employer sponsored plan that establishes accounts for employees where they can deposit pre-tax payroll deductions for the purpose of either medical care, dependent care, or both.

formulary   A list of drugs created by an insurance company that will be covered by an insurance plan, possibly at a lower co-payment amount.

gap insurance   A policy or combination of policies that fills in the difference between the coverage allowed by the HDHP and the savings allowed in the HSA.

generic drug   A drug that is not manufactured by the original patent holder, but is chemically identical to its brand name counterpart.

HDHP   *See* High Deductible Health Plan.

HDMP   High Deductible Medical Plan, alternate name for HDHP.

health-care Flexible Spending Account   An employer sponsored account where employees can deposit pre-tax earnings for the purpose of medical expenses. Unused funds revert to the employer at the end of the plan year.

Health Insurance Portability and Accountability Act of 1996 (HIPAA)   Federal law which prohibits pre-existing conditions clauses in certain group contracts and restricts the disclosure of private health information.

health maintenance organization   A group of medical providers who provide services to members through pre-paid contracts, which guarantee the availability of care within the group (or network) of providers.

Health Savings Account   A tax status given to a variety of savings and investment vehicles which allows tax deferred deposits up to stated yearly limits, tax-deferred interest, and tax-free withdrawals for qualified medical expenses.

Health Savings Security Account (HSSA)   A proposed account that did not pass into law that would have allowed a savings account without an accompanying insurance plan.

High Deductible Health Plan (HDHP)   A health insurance plan offered by insurance companies, qualified by the IRS to allow an insured to open and make deposits to a Health Savings Account.

home health care   Medical services that are delivered to or provided in a patient's home.

HSA   See *Health Savings Account*.

in-network   Refers to providers that have signed contracts to provide services at an agreed upon rate to insured individuals of a specific insurance company.

indemnity plans   A type of group health insurance that pays the same reimbursement to all providers, or pays based on a usual and customary charge standard rate.

index   A factor derived from some agreed upon calculation that is applied to another number to adjust it (e.g., Consumer Price Index).

individual deductible   The amount of covered services that must be paid by the insured for him- or herself at 100 percent before the insurance company begins reimbursing any expenses.

individual underwriting   The process an insurance company completes to assess the risk of accepting an applicant for health insurance coverage. It includes reviewing specific medical questions and requesting doctors' statements.

Individual Retirement Account   A tax-deferred status applied to a variety of investment and savings vehicles for the purpose of encouraging individuals to accumulate money for retirement.

inpatient care   Medical services received while confined in a hospital or other care facility.

insurance commissioner   Person appointed by each state to run that state's Department of Insurance (or counterpart), which regulates the insurance industry in that state.

Internal Revenue Service (IRS)   Part of the United States Department of the Treasury, charged with collecting income and other taxes.

lifetime maximum   The stated amount in a health-insurance contract that is the most that can be paid while insured under that contract.

long-term care   Custodial services needed to conduct the activities of daily living.

long-term care insurance   A policy that pays for a portion of the costs of long-term care, in a nursing home or possibly in the patient's home.

managed care   A system of cost containment used by insurance companies and health maintenance organizations including such strategies as preauthorization, use of primary-care providers, and provider utilization review.

maximum annual benefit   The most a health-insurance policy will pay in any given year.

Medical Savings Accounts (Archer MSAs)
An earlier tax-advantaged savings accounts with limited eligibility and availability, compared to HSAs.

money market mutual fund   A short-term investment that pools investor's money into short-term debt instruments, such as CD's and Treasury Bills.

negotiated fees   The contractual amount that an insurance company will pay to a network provider for stated medical services.

network   A group of medical service providers who have signed contracts with a specific insurance company to provide services for negotiated fees, usually discounted from their usual fees.

noncancellable policy   A policy that guarantees you can continue to receive benefits as long as you pay your premium.

nonformulary   Refers to a drug in not included in the insurance company's formulary list.

office visit   An appointment between a patient and his or her physician at the physician's office or other facility.

Old Age, Survivors, Disability and Health Insurance (OASDHI)   The official term for the package of government run insurance benefits commonly and collectively called Social Security.

open enrollment   The one or two month period during each plan year (usually the first and/or last) when an employee may elect coverage in a health plan if they did not join when they were eligible after hiring.

out-of-area benefits   Refers to the level of reimbursement provided for insurers living outside the service area of a network based health-insurance plan.

out-of-network provider   A medical services provider that has not signed a contract with a specific insurance company.

out-of-pocket maximum   The amount of expense incurred by an insured that when reached causes the insurance company to then pick up 100 percent of the expenses. May include the deductible in the number, as in the case of High Deductible Health Plans.

outpatient care   Medical services received in a hospital or other care facility which take fewer hours and do no not require an overnight stay or incur room and board charges.

point-of-service plan (POS)   A health insurance plan that requires a primary care physician to manage the insured's care and refer to specialists. Usually includes office visit co-payments and low deductibles.

portable   Refers to the ability to retain a benefit after terminating employment. Health Savings Accounts are portable because of the fact that they are titled to the employee.

pre-certification   The sometimes required process during which an insurance company reviews medical services and their costs prior to the service being completed.

pre-existing condition   A medical condition that was treated or diagnosed in a stated period (often six months) prior to the start of coverage on a new health-insurance policy.

pre-existing conditions clause   A feature of many health-insurance policies that excludes coverage for pre-existing conditions for a specific period (often one year.) This clause is waived on group plans for those who had other group coverage not more than 63 days earlier per the HIPAA rules.

Preferred Provider Organization (PPO) A group of medical care providers who have contracted to provide their services to a specific insurance company at a negotiate rate.

Preferred Provider Organization Plan   An insurance contract that reimburses at different rates for services provided by a PPO member versus services provided by others.

premium   The amount paid, usually on a monthly basis, to an insurance company in exchange for coverage by a health-insurance contract.

pre-tax contributions   Deposits made to a Health Savings Accounts through payroll deduction arrangements, using money not taxed by the federal, state, and local governments. A deduction cannot be taken when filing federal taxes for these deposits.

pre-tax premiums   Deposits made to a Health Savings Accounts through payroll deduction arrangements, using money not taxed by the federal, state, and local governments. A deduction cannot be taken when filing federal taxes for these deposits.

preventive care   Medical services offered to well individuals to help maintain health and predict possible health risks.

primary-care physician   A medical practitioner required by some health-insurance plans to manage the care of insured and refer to other specialists, when needed.

provider   A person, company or institution that delivers medical care.

Qualified High Deductible Health Plan (QHDHP)   Used to refer to plans that permit individuals to open an HSA. QHDHP and HDHP are often used interchangeably.

qualified withdrawal   Removal of money from a Health Savings Account in accordance with Internal Revenue Service rules that do not invoke any taxes or penalties. See list in Appendix B.

qualifying event   Refers to an event that allows an individual to elect coverage under a group plan or continue coverage under COBRA rules (e.g., marriage, divorce, death, termination).

reallocation   Changing the selection of investments in your portfolio of assets.

reasonable and customary charges   The rate normally charged by the market in the geographic area where the patient is receiving services.

residential treatment   Medical care provided in a 24-hour setting that is less comprehensive than hospital care.

risk pool   A group of insured policyholders who purchase same or similar policy types to combine their probability of loss.

rollover HSA   A Health Savings Account that has received funds from an existing Medical Savings Account or Health Savings Account.

Section 125 Plan   *See* Flexible Spending Account.

short-term investment   An investment used to fund needs in the next year, usually with stable but lower rates of return than other investment choices.

specialist   A medical practitioner who treats only certain parts of the body or types of illnesses.

urgent care   Medical services received for critical illnesses and injuries outside of an emergency room.

third-party administrator   Company licensed to do a variety of health insurance related activities, such as actuarial calculations, claims payments, and enrollments.

trustee   The financial institution that holds the Health Savings Account funds and is required to provide certain tax reporting each year.

vesting   Refers to the level of ownership by employees in a company-sponsored plan. Health Savings Accounts are immediately vested, even if funded in full by the employer.

waive   Give up a right or contract provision, as in waiving a pre-existing conditions clause.

well-baby care   Medical services provided to infants and toddlers that is primarily preventive care.

Tax Forms

Publication 502—Tax Deductible Withdrawals

Following is a list of items that can be paid for with withdrawals from your Health Savings Account without tax or penalty. They can be paid on behalf of yourself, your spouse, and your dependents. The items are listed in alphabetical order. A more detailed explanation of each item is available from the Internal Revenue Service in section 213(d) of the Internal Revenue Code.

Abortion

Acupuncture

Alcoholism

Ambulance

Artificial limb

Artificial teeth

Bandages

Breast reconstruction surgery

Birth control pills

Braille books and magazines (additional expense)

Capital expenses to accommodate medical conditions (not including the increased value of your home)

Car (additional expense to accommodate medical condition)

Chiropractor

Christian science practitioner

Contact lenses and cleaners

Crutches

Dental treatment

Diagnostic devices

Disabled dependent care expenses

Drug addiction

Drugs

Eyeglasses

Eye surgery

Fertility enhancement

Guide dog or other animal

Health institute

Hearing aids

Home care

Hospital services

Insurance premiums

Group health insurance during COBRA period

Individual health insurance while unemployed

Parts A, B, D and HMO Medicare premiums

Qualified long-term care insurance contracts (subject to additional limitations)

Laboratory fees

Lead-based paint removal

Learning disability

Legal fees necessary to authorize medical treatment

Lodging necessary to receive medical care

Long-term care

Maintenance of chronically ill individual

Meals (at medical facilities while receiving inpatient care)

Medical conferences (concerning family illnesses)

Medical information plan

Medical services

Physicians

Surgeons

Specialists

Other medical practitioners

Medicines, prescription and nonprescription

Mentally retarded, special home for

Nursing home

Nursing services

Optometrist

Organ donors

Osteopath

Oxygen

Prosthesis

Psychiatric care

Psychoanalysis

Psychologist

Special education for learning disabilities caused by mental or physical impairment

Sterilization

Stop-smoking programs (except nonprescription drugs)

Surgery

Telephone adaptations for hearing impaired person

Television adaptations for hearing impaired person

Therapy

Transplants, donating or receiving

Transportation needed for medical care

Trips for medical reasons

Vasectomy

Vision correction surgery

Weight-loss program, excepting food, for the specific treatment of a diagnosed condition

Wheelchair

Wig, needed due to disease

X-ray

What Expenses Are Not Deductible?

The following is a list of some items that you cannot fund from your Health Savings Accounts without penalty. This list would include everything not listed above, such as big screen TV's, but for the sake of space only includes those items that people might mistake for deductible items. The items are listed in alphabetical order.

Baby sitting, childcare, and nursing services for a normal, healthy baby

Controlled substances

Cosmetic surgery, unless directly related to disease

Dancing, swimming, or other lessons

Diaper service, unless needed due to disease

Electrolysis or hair removal

Funeral expenses

Future medical care, except long term care contracts

Hair transplant

Health club dues

Household help

Illegal operations and treatments

Insurance premiums, except those listed above

Maternity clothes

Medicines and drugs from other countries

Nutritional supplements, if prescribed for a specific medical condition

Personal use items

Teeth whitening

Veterinary fees, except for the care of guide and assist dogs

Form 1099-SA

Most people are familiar with 1099—they cover a variety of income sources and other taxable transactions. The 1099-SA (Savings Account) is used to report the money withdrawn from a Health Savings Account during a given tax year. As long as the withdrawals were for qualified expenses (see Internal Revenue Code section 213[d]) there will be no income tax or penalty imposed.

	CORRECTED (if checked)			
TRUSTEE'S/PAYER'S name, street address, city, state, and ZIP code		OMB No. 1545-1517 2005 Form **1099-SA**		Distributions From an HSA, Archer MSA, or Medicare Advantage MSA
PAYER'S Federal identification number	RECIPIENT'S identification number	1 Gross distribution $	2 Earnings on excess cont. $	Copy B For Recipient
RECIPIENT'S name		3 Distribution code	4 FMV on date of death $	
Street address (including apt. no.)		5 HSA ☐ Archer MSA ☐ MA MSA ☐		This information is being furnished to the Internal Revenue Service.
City, state, and ZIP code				
Account number (see instructions)				
Form **1099-SA**		(keep for your records)	Department of the Treasury - Internal Revenue Service	

Form 5498-SA

This form will report your contributions to an HSA during the year. It may help you to complete your form 8889, but is not issued until after your tax return would normally be due.

Form 8889

This is the worksheet that helps you to determine your maximum contribution allowed for the tax year and reports your contributions and distributions for the year. Any deduction you would need to claim will carry forward from this form to line 28 of the 1040.

Form **8889**

Department of the Treasury
Internal Revenue Service

Health Savings Accounts (HSAs)

► Attach to Form 1040.   ► See separate instructions.

OMB No. 1545-0074

20**05**

Attachment
Sequence No. **138**

Name(s) shown on Form 1040

Social security number of HSA
beneficiary. If both spouses have
HSAs, see page 2 of the instructions ►

Before you begin: Complete Form 8853, Archer MSAs and Long-Term Care Insurance Contracts, if required.

Part I — **HSA Contributions and Deduction.** See page 2 of the instructions before completing this part. If you are filing jointly and both you and your spouse each have separate HSAs, complete a separate Part I for each spouse (see page 2 of the instructions).

1	Check the box to indicate your coverage under a high-deductible health plan (HDHP) during 2005 (see page 2 of the instructions) . . . . ►	☐ Self-only ☐ Family	
2	HSA contributions you made for 2005 (or those made on your behalf), including those made from January 1, 2006, through April 17, 2006, that were for 2005. **Do not** include employer contributions or rollovers (see page 2 of the instructions)	**2**	
3	If you were under age 55 at the end of 2005, and on the first day of **every** month during 2005, you were an eligible individual with the **same** annual deductible and coverage, enter the *smaller* of: • Your annual deductible (see page 2 of the instructions), or • $2,650 ($5,250 for family coverage). All others, enter the limit from the worksheet on page 3 of the instructions	**3**	
4	Enter the amount you and your employer contributed to your Archer MSAs for 2005 from Form 8853, lines 3 and 4. If you or your spouse had family coverage under an HDHP at any time during 2005, also include any amount contributed to your spouse's Archer MSAs	**4**	
5	Subtract line 4 from line 3. If zero or less, enter -0-	**5**	
6	Enter the amount from line 5. But if you and your spouse each have separate HSAs and had family coverage under an HDHP at any time during 2005, see the instructions on page 3 for the amount to enter.	**6**	
7	If you were age 55 or older at the end of 2005, married, and you or your spouse had family coverage under an HDHP at any time during 2005, enter your additional contribution amount (see page 4 of the instructions)	**7**	
8	Add lines 6 and 7	**8**	
9	Employer contributions made to your HSAs for 2005	**9**	
10	Subtract line 9 from line 8. If zero or less, enter -0-	**10**	
11	**HSA deduction.** Enter the *smaller* of line 2 or line 10 here and on Form 1040, line 25 **Caution:** *If line 2 is more than line 11, you may have to pay an additional tax (see page 4 of the instructions).*	**11**	

Part II — **HSA Distributions.** If you are filing jointly and both you and your spouse each have separate HSAs, complete a separate Part II for each spouse.

12a	Total distributions you received in 2005 from all HSAs (see page 4 of the instructions) . .	**12a**	
b	Distributions included on line 12a that you rolled over to another HSA. Also include any excess contributions (and the earnings on those excess contributions) included on line 12a that were withdrawn by the due date of your return (see page 4 of the instructions)	**12b**	
c	Subtract line 12b from line 12a	**12c**	
13	Unreimbursed qualified medical expenses (see page 4 of the instructions)	**13**	
14	**Taxable HSA distributions.** Subtract line 13 from line 12c. If zero or less, enter -0-. Also, include this amount in the total on Form 1040, line 21. On the dotted line next to line 21, enter "HSA" and the amount	**14**	
15a	If any of the distributions included on line 14 meet any of the **Exceptions to the Additional 10% Tax** (see page 5 of the instructions), check here . . . . ► ☐		
b	**Additional 10% tax** (see page 5 of the instructions). Enter 10% (.10) of the distributions included on line 14 that are subject to the additional 10% tax. Also include this amount in the total on Form 1040, line 63. On the dotted line next to line 63, enter "HSA" and the amount . . .	**15b**	

For Paperwork Reduction Act Notice, see page 5 of the instructions.   Cat. No. 37621P   Form **8889** (2005)

HDHP Providers

Here is a listing of 25 of the major insurance companies offering High Deductible Health Plans. Some of them only offer group coverage. Some offer just individual coverage. And others offer both. Some will also sell you an HSA along with your HDHP. I have listed the states where they are licensed, but they may not have all of their products approved in all states.

Aetna
151 Farmington Avenue
Hartford, CT 06156
860-273-0123, www.aetna.com
Doing business in: AZ, CA, CO, CT, DC, DE, FL, GA, IL, IN, MD, ME, NJ, NY, OH, OK, OR, PA, TX, VA, KY
Products: Individual, Group, HSA

American Community Mutual Insurance Company
39201 Seven Mile Road
Livonia, MI 48152-1094
1-800-991-2642, www.american-community.com
Doing business in: AZ, IL, IN, IA, MI, MO, NE, OH, PA
Products: Individual, Group

American National
2302 Postoffice Street, Suite 601
Galveston, TX 77550
1-800-252-4002, www.anico.com
Doing business in: AR, AZ, DE, IA, IL, LA, MI,
MO, NC, NE, OH, OK, PA, SC, TN, TX, VA,
WI, WY
Products: Individual, HSA

American Republic Insurance Company
601 6th Avenue
Des Moines, IA 50309
1-800-247-2190, www.americanrepublic.com
Doing business in: AL, AZ, CO, CT, IL, IN, IA,
MO, NE, NH, NM, NC, OH, OK, PA, SC, TN,
VA, WI
Products: Individual

Anthem
120 Monument Circle
Indianapolis, IN 46204
1-888-641-5224, www.anthem.com
Doing business in: IN, KY, OH, CT, NH, CO,
NV, ME, VA
Products: Individual, Group

Assurant Health
501 West Michigan
Milwaukee, WI 53201
1-800-800-1212, www.assuranthealth.com
Doing business in: AL, AK, AZ, AR, CA, CO, CT,
DC, DE, FL, GA, ID, IL, IN, IA, KS, KY, LA,
MD, MI, MN, MS, MO, MT, NE, NV, NH, NM,
NC, ND, OH, OK, OR, PA, SC, SD, TN, TX,
UT, VA, WV, WI, WY
Products: Individual, Group, HSA

Celtic
233 S. Wacker Dr., Ste. 700
Chicago, IL 60606
1-800-477-7870, www.celtic-net.com
Doing business in: AK, AL, AZ, CO, CT, DE, DC,
GA, IA, IL, IN, KS, LA, MI, MO, MS, MT, NE,
NC, NH, NM, OK, PA, SC, SD, TN, TX,
WV, WI, WY
Products: Individual, HSA

Central Reserve Life Insurance Company
17800 Royalton Road
Cleveland, OH 44136
1-800-321-3997, www.centralreserve.com
Doing business in: AL, AZ, IL, IN, MO, NE, OH,
OK, PA, TN, VA, WV, WI
Products: Individual, Group, HSA

Cigna
One Liberty Place 1650 Market Street
Philadelphia, PA 19192
1-800-832-3211, www.cignachoicefund.com
Doing business in: AL, AK, AZ, AR, CA, CO, CT,
DE, DC, FL, GA, ID, IL, IN, IA, KS, KY, LA,
ME, MD, MA, MI, MN, MS, MO, MT, NE, NV,
NH, NJ, NM, NY, NC, ND, OH, OK, OR, PA,
RI, SC, SD, TN, TX, UT, VT, VA, WA, WV,
WI, WY
Products: Group, HSA

Continental General Insurance Company
8901 Indian Hills Drive
Omaha, NE 68124
1-800-545-8905, www.continentalgeneral.com
Doing business in: AL, AZ, DE, FL, GA, IA, IL,
IN, MI, MO, NE, NV, OH, OK, PA, SC, TN, VA,
WI, WV
Products: Individual

Corporate Benefit Service of America, Inc.
400 Highway 169 South, Suite 800
Minneapolis, MN 55426-1141
1-800-765-4224, www.cbsainc.com
Doing business in: AZ, AR, GA, ID, IL, IN, IA,
LA, MS, MO, MT, NE, NV, NM, NC, OH, OK,
SC, SD, TN, TX, WI, WY
Products: Group, HSA

Freedom HSA
8009 34th Ave. S., Ste. 360
Bloomington, MN 55425
1-866-746-6610, www.FreedomHSA.org
Doing business in: AZ, CO, IL, IN, IA, KS, MI,
MO, MT, NE, NM, ND, OH, OK, SD, TN, TX,
WI, WY
Products: Individual, HSA

Golden Rule
712 Eleventh Street
Lawrenceville, IL 62439
1-800-444-8990, www.goldenrule.com
Doing business in: AL, AK, AZ, AR, CO, CT, DE,
DC, FL, GA, IL, IN, IA, MD, MI, MS, MO, NE,
OH, OK, PA, SC, TN, TX, VA, WV, WIAL
Products: Individual, HSA

Great West Healthcare
8505 E. Orchard Rd.
Greenwood Village, CO 80111
1-866-442-3890, www.greatwesthealthcare.com
Doing business in: AL, AK, AZ, AR, CA, CO, CT,
DE, DC, FL, GA, ID, IL, IN, IA, KS, KY, LA,
ME, MD, MA, MI, MN, MS, MO, MT, NE, NV,
NH, NJ, NM, NY, NC, ND, OH, OK, OR, PA,
RI, SC, SD, TN, TX, UT, VT, VA, WA, WV,
WI, WY
Products: Group, HSA

John Alden Life Insurance Company
501 West Michigan
Milwaukee, WI 53201
414-271-3011, www.nstarmarketing.com
Doing business in: AL, AK, AZ, AR, CA, CO, CT,
DE, DC, FL, GA, ID, IL, IN, IA, KS, KY, LA,
MD, MI, MN, MS, MO, MT, NE, NV, NH, NM,
NC, ND, OH, OK, OR, PA, SC, SD, TN, TX,
UT, VA, WV, WI, WY
Products: Individual, Group, HSA

Medical Mutual
2060 East 9th Street
Cleveland, OH 44115
1-800-700-2583, www.medmutual.com
Doing business in: OH, IN, MI, PA, WV
Products: Individual, Group

Medical Savings Health Plan
5835 W. 74th Street P.O. Box 68961
Indianapolis, IN 46268-0961
1-888-696-9663, www.medicalsavings.com
Doing business in: CA, FL, IL, IN, NE, OH, SC, VA, WV
Products: Individual, HSA

MMA Stewardship Solutions
1110 North Main Street PO Box 483
Goshen, IN 46527
1-800-348-7468, www.mma-online.org
Doing business in: AZ, IL, IN, IA, KS, MD, MI, MT, NE, OH, OK, OR, PA, SD, VA
Products: Individual, Group, HSA

Mutual of Omaha
Mutual of Omaha Plaza
Omaha, NE 68175
402-342-7600, www.mutualofomaha.com
Doing business in: AK, AZ, CO, GA ID, IL, IA, KS, MO, MT, NE, NV, NM, NC, OK, OR, TX, WA
Products: Group, HSA

PacifiCare Health Systems
3100 AMS Boulevard PO Box 19032
Green Bay, WI 54307-9032
1-800-232-5432, www.eams.com
Doing business in: AZ, AR, CO, DE, FL, GA, IL, IN, KS, LA, MI, MO, NC, NE, NM, OH, OK, PA, SC, TX, UT, VA, WI, WV, GA
Products: Individual

Principal Financial Group
711 High Street
Des Moines, IA 50392-0001
1-800-986-3343, www.principal.com
Doing business in: GA, IA, IL, IN, MI, MO, OH,
TN, TX, WI
Products: Group, HSA

Starmark
400 Field Drive
Lake Forest, IL 60045
1-800-522-1246, www.starmarkinc.com/starmark/
Doing business in: AK, AZ, AR, DE, DC, GA, ID,
IL, IN, IA, KS, LA, MI, MS, MO, MT, NE, NH,
NV, NM, NC, OH, OK, PA, SC, TN, TX, UT,
VA, WV, WI, WY
Products: Group

Unicare
Two Constitution Plaza, 2nd Floor
Charlestown, MA 02129
617-580-2000, www.unicare.com
Doing business in: AL, AK, AZ, AR, CA, CO, CT,
DE, DC, FL, GA, HI, ID, IL, IN, IA, KS, KY, LA,
ME, MD, MA, MI, MN, MS, MO, MT, NE, NV,
NH, NJ, NM, NY, NC, ND, OH, OK, OR, PA,
RI, SC, SD, TN, TX, UT, VT, VA, WA, WV,
WI, WY
Products: Individual, Group, HSA

UnitedHealthcare
1600 Utica Avenue South, Suite 900
St. Louis Park, MN 55416
952-277-5000, www.definityhealth.com
Doing business in: AL, AK, AZ, AR, CA, CO, CT,
DE, DC, FL, GA, HI, ID, IL, IN, IA, KS, KY, LA,
ME, MD, MA, MI, MN, MS, MO, MT, NE, NV,
NH, NJ, NM, NY, NC, ND, OH, OK, OR, PA,
RI, SC, SD, TN, TX, UT, VT, VA, WA, WV,
WI, WY
Products: Individual, Group, HSA

HSA Providers

The following is a partial listing of early entrants into the HSA market. These trustees are doing business outside of their hometowns via mail and the Internet. You do not need to have your HDHP with a particular insurance company to open an account with most of them.

American Chartered Bank
932 West Randolph Street
Chicago, IL 60607
847-517-5400
www.americanchartered.com

The Bancorp Bank HSA
405 Silverside Road, Suite 105
Wilmington, DE 19809
1-800-555-9316
www.thebancorphsa.com

Bank of Cashton
723 Main Street
Cashton, WI 54619
608-654-5121
www.bankofcashton.com

Bank of Oak Ridge
2211 Oak Ridge Road
Oak Ridge, NC 27310
336-644-9944
www.bankofoakridge.com

Blackhawk Bank
200 Broad Street
Beloit, WI 53511
1-866-771-8924
www.blackhawkbank.com

Capitol Bank
710 North High Point Road
Madison, WI 53717
608-836-1616
www.capitolbank.com

Cattle National Bank & Trust Company
104 South Fifth Street
Seward, NE 68434
402-643-3636
www.cattlebank.com

Citywide Banks
6500 East Hampden Avenue
Denver, CO 80224
303-365-3650
www.citywidebanks.com

Equity Trust Co.
225 Burns Road
Elyria, OH 44035
440-323-5491
www.trustetc.com/hsa/hsa.html

Exante Bank
PO Box 271629
Salt Lake City, UT 84127
1-866-234-8913
www.exantebankhsa.com

HealthAmerica Credit Union
9790 Touchton Road
Jacksonville, FL 32246
1-866-317-4228
www.healthamericaca.com

Fifth Third Bank
38 Fountain Square
Cincinnati, OH 45263
1-800-972-3030
www.53.com

First American Bank
1650 Louis Avenue
Elk Grove Village, IL 60007
847-952-3700 x Opt 2 & 3
www.firstambank.com

First HSA
1044 MacArthur Road
Reading, PA 19605
1-888-769-8696
www.firstmsa.com

Health Savings Administrators, LLC
10800 Midlothian Turnpike, Suite 240
Richmond, VA 23235
1-888-354-0697
www.hsaadministrators.com

HSA Bank
605 North Eighth Street, Suite 320
Sheboygan, WI 53081
1-800-357-6246
www.hsabank.com

HSA Resources Bank
PO Box 7338
St. Cloud MN 56302
1-888-343-4422
www.hsaresourcesbank.com

hsa Trustee Services
611 West Main Street
PO Box 1088
Lake Geneva, WI 53147
1-866-472-2010
www.hsatrusteeservices.com

Mid-America Bank HSA
802 Ames
Baldwin City, KS 66006
785-594-2100
www.mabhsa.com

MSaver Bank
7400 West 110th Street, Suite 520
Overland Park, KS 66210
1-888-367-6727
www.msaver.com

Professional Bank N.A.
2101 Abrams Road
Dallas, TX 75214
214-269-2100
www.professionalbankna.com

Resource Bank
5100 Village Walk, Suite 102
Covington, LA 70433
985-612-3000
www.resourcebk.com

Saturna Capital
1300 North State Street
Bellingham, WA 98225
1-800-728-8762
www.saturna.com

Sherman County Bank
734 'O' Street
Loup City, NE 68853
308-745-1500
www.shermancountybank.com

Southwestern National Bank
6901 Corporate Drive
Houston, Texas 77036
713-995-3226
www.southwesternnationalbank.com

State Farm Bank
PO Box 2316
Bloomington, IL 61702
1-877-734-2265
www.statefarm.com/bank/hsa.htm

Thrivent Financial Bank
2000 East Milestone Drive
Appleton, WI 54919
1-866-226-5225
www.thrivent.com/bank/hsa/index.html

Thoroughbred Health Bank
120 West Canadian
Vinita, OK 74301
1-800-806-5033
www.thoroughbredhealth.com

Tower Bank & Trust Company
116 East Berry Street
Fort Wayne, IN 46802
260-427-7007
www.towerbank.net

Town Bank
400 Genesee Street
Delafield, WI 53018
1-800-433-3076
www.townbank.us

Town Center Bank
10413 SE 82nd Avenue
Portland, OR 97266
503-788-8181
www.towncenterbank.com

U.S. Bank
800 Nicollet Mall
Minneapolis, MN 55402
1-877-472-6789
http://healthsavings.usbank.com

Westfield Bank
Two Park Circle
Westfield Center, OH 44251
1-800-368-8930
www.westfield-bank.com

Appendix E

State Insurance Departments

State	Web Address/ Phone Number
Alabama	www.aldoi.org/ 334-269-3550
Alaska	www.dced.state.ak.us/insurance/ 907-465-2515
Arizona	www.id.state.az.us/ 1-800-325-2548
Arkansas	www.state.ar.us/insurance/ 1-800-282-9134
California	www.insurance.ca.gov/docs/ 1-800-927-HELP
Colorado	www.dora.state.co.us/insurance/ 1-800-930-3745
Connecticut	www.ct.gov/cid/ 1-800-203-3447
Delaware	www.state.de.us/inscom/ 1-800-282-8611
Washington D.C.	dc.gov/agencies/ 202-727-8000

State	Web Address/ Phone Number
Florida	www.fldfs.com/companies/ 1-800-342-2762
Georgia	www.gainsurance.org/ 1-800-656-2298
Hawaii	www.state.hi.us/dcca/ins/ 808-586-2790
Idaho	www.doi.state.id.us/ 1-800-721-3272
Illinois	www.idfpr.com/DOI/ 1-877-527-9431
Indiana	www.in.gov/idoi/ 317-232-2385
Iowa	www.iid.state.ia.us/ 1-877-955-1212
Kansas	www.ksinsurance.org 1-800-432-2484
Kentucky	www.doi.state.ky.us/ 1-800-595-6053
Louisiana	www.ldi.la.gov/ 1-800-259-5300
Maine	www.state.me.us/pfr/ins/ 1-800-300-5000
Maryland	www.mdinsurance.state.md.us 1-800-492-6116
Massachusetts	www.mass.gov/doi/ 617-521-7794
Michigan	www.michigan.gov/cis/ 1-877-999-6442
Minnesota	www.commerce.state.mn.us/ 1-800-657-3602

State	Web Address/ Phone Number
Mississippi	www.ms.gov 1-800-562-2957
Missouri	www.insurance.state.mo.us/ 1-800-762-7390
Montana	www.discoveringmontana.com/sao/ 1-800-332-6148
Nebraska	www.doi.ne.gov/ 1-877-564-7323
Nevada	www.doi.state.nv.us/ 775-687-4270
New Hampshire	www.state.nh.us/insurance 1-800-852-3416
New Jersey	www.state.nj.us/dobi/ 1-800-446-7467
New Mexico	www.nmprc.state.nm.us/ insurance/inshm.htm 1-800-947-4722
New York	www.ins.state.ny.us 1-800-342-3736
North Carolina	www.ncdoi.com 1-800-546-5664
North Dakota	www.state.nd.us/ndins 1-800-247-0560
Ohio	www.ohioinsurance.gov/ 1-800-686-1526
Oklahoma	www.oid.state.ok.us/ 1-800-522-0071
Oregon	www.cbs.state.or.us/external/ins 503-947-7980
Pennsylvania	www.insurance.state.pa.us/ 1-877-881-6388

State	Web Address/ Phone Number
Puerto Rico	www.ocs.gobierno.pr/ 787-722-8686
Rhode Island	www.dbr.state.ri.us 401-222-2246
South Carolina	www.doi.state.sc.us/ 1-800-768-3467
South Dakota	www.state.sd.us/drr/reg/insurance 605-773-3563
Tennessee	www.state.tn.us/commerce/ 615-741-4737
Texas	www.tdi.state.tx.us 1-800-252-3439
Utah	www.insurance.state.ut.us 1-800-439-3805
Vermont	www.bishca.state.vt.us 802-828-3301
Virginia	www.scc.virginia.gov 1-800-552-7945
Washington	www.insurance.wa.gov 1-800-562-6900
West Virginia	www.wvinsurance.gov 1-888-879-9842
Wisconsin	www.oci.wi.gov 1-800-236-8517
Wyoming	insurance.state.wy.us/ 1-800-438-5768

Resources

www.AMBest.com

The oldest, most respected independent rating service for insurance companies.

A.M. Best Company, Inc.
Ambest Road
Oldwick, NJ 08858
908-439-2200

www.irs.gov

The Internal Revenue website for access to forms and publications needed to service Health Savings Accounts.

Internal Revenue Service—Business Assistance
1-800-829-4933

www.ustreas.gov/offices/public-affairs/hsa/

The United States Treasury website, which posts all official rulings regarding HSAs.

United States Treasury
1500 Pennsylvania Avenue, NW
Washington, D.C. 20220
202-622-2000

www.ahrq.gov

The United States Department of Health and Human Services website, which provides research on health care and health insurance.

Agency for Healthcare Research and Quality
540 Gaither Road
Rockville, MD 30850
301-427-1364

www.hsainsider.com

HSAInsider is a service of the HSA Coalition, a group of nonprofit organizations and businesses that advocates for affordable health care. It provides information and links to insurance companies and banks.

The HSA Insider
2121 K Street NW, Suite 800
Washington, D.C. 20037
202-558-2303

www.hsadecisions.org

Americas Health Insurance Plans (AHIP) is a
trade association representing health insurance
companies. The website includes an online
Learning Center regarding HSA options.

America's Health Insurance Plans
601 Pennsylvania Avenue NW
South Building, Suite 500
Washington, D.C. 20004
202-778-3200

www.hsafinder.com

A service of a marketing research firm that collects
information on health care issues.

Information Strategies, Inc.
PO Box 563
Palisades Park, NJ 07650
customerservice@hsafinder.com

www.nahu.org/consumer/HSAGuide.htm

A consumer's guide to HSAs published by the trade
association for health insurance brokers in the
United States.

National Association of Health Underwriters
2000 North 14th Street, Suite 450
Arlington, VA 22201
703-276-0220

www.ahia.net/consumers/guide_hsa.html

A consumers guide developed by the health insurance division of the National Association of Insurance and Financial Advisors.

Association of Health Insurance Advisors
2901 Telestar Court
Falls Church, VA 22042-1205
703-770-8200

www.naabc.com

A trade association of brokers and consultants specializing in Consumer Directed Health Care approaches.

National Association of Alternative Benefit Consultants
435 Pennsylvania Avenue
Glen Ellyn, IL 60137
1-800-627-0552

Index

I-J